SIMPLICITY, SPIRITUALITY, SERVICE

# Simplicity, Spirituality, Service

*The Timeless Wisdom of Francis, Clare, and Bonaventure*

Bruce G. Epperly

**franciscan**
media®
Cincinnati, Ohio

Selection from *Francis and Clare: The Complete Works*, translation and introduction by Regis Armstrong, OFM Cap,, and Ignatius C. Brady, OFM, Copyright © 1986 by Paulist Press, Inc., New York/Mahwah, NJ. Reprinted by permission of Paulist Press, Inc. www.paulistpress.com. Excerpts from *Francis of Assisi: Early Documents*, edited by Regis J. Armstrong, J.A. Wayne Hellmann and William J. Short, copyright ©1999. Reprinted with permission of New City Press. Scripture quotations are from *New Revised Standard Version Bible*, copyright © 1989 National Council of the Churches of Christ in the United States of America. Used by permission. All rights reserved worldwide.

LIBRARY OF CONGRESS CATALOGING-IN-PUBLICATION DATA
Names: Epperly, Bruce Gordon, author.
Title: Simplicity, spirituality, service : the timeless wisdom of Francis, Clare, and Bonaventure / Bruce G. Epperly.
Description: Cincinnati, Ohio : Franciscan Media, [2023] | Includes bibliographical references. | Summary: "The wisdom of the early Franciscan saints-Francis, Clare, and Bonaventure-continues to resonate in the thinking and spirituality of many in the twenty-first century. Their approach to life can lead us to new solutions to the chaos of our time as well as new ways to appreciate and celebrate the joy of God's creation, human and nonhuman alike"-- Provided by publisher.
Identifiers: LCCN 2023025380 (print) | LCCN 2023025381 (ebook) | ISBN 9781632534422 (trade paperback) | ISBN 9781632534446 (ebook)
Subjects: LCSH: Spiritual life--Christianity. | Franciscans--Spiritual life. | Francis, of Assisi, Saint, 1182-1226. | Clare, of Assisi, Saint, 1194-1253. | Bonaventure, Saint, Cardinal, approximately 1217-1274.
Classification: LCC BV4501.3 .E675 2023  (print) | LCC BV4501.3  (ebook) | DDC 248.4--dc23/eng/20230719
LC record available at https://lccn.loc.gov/2023025380
LC ebook record available at https://lccn.loc.gov/2023025381

ISBN 978-1-63253-442-2

Cover design by Frank Gutbrod
Book design by Mark Sullivan

To my grandchildren and the children of the world:
May you be always new, always fresh,
and always beginning again.
*Ubuntu,* "I am because of you" and
"We will become because we are together."

CONTENTS

The steadfast love of the Lord never ceases,

God's mercies never come to an end;

they are new every morning;

great is your faithfulness.

—LAMENTATIONS 3:22–23

Francis was always new, always fresh, always beginning again.

—THOMAS OF CELANO[1]

Unexpected moments can change our lives: moments when we receive a message, word, image, or inclination that points us in a new direction, reveals fresh possibilities, and initiates an unplanned adventure. These inspirational moments can come through a chance encounter, a post on social media, or a surprise phone call. Unexpected insights and events regularly inspire my vocation as a writer and teacher, reminding me to begin again with fresh and creative ideas, and the origin of this book is no exception. I received a surprising message from the nonhuman world as I took my morning walk in the Washington, DC, suburb I call home.

The publishing team at Franciscan Media had asked me to consider writing a sequel to *Walking with Francis of Assisi: From Privilege to Activism,* focusing on the spiritual resources of Franciscan spirituality for twenty-first-century life, and I was getting nowhere. I had sent a proposal, but initially, it felt more like an assignment I needed to complete, a box to check in my writer's journey, than the result of joyful passion, and I felt intellectually stalled. For several days, I had prayerfully contemplated questions such as, *Should I go ahead with the book project, or say no to the generous offer from Franciscan Media? What would I have to say that would change my life in the process of study and writing and also contribute to the spiritual growth of my readers? Am I experiencing God's vision, God's passion, moving in and through my own passion and vision as I contemplate writing this book?*

Then, much to my surprise and delight, and without any effort on my part, I found an answer. As I walked in my tree-lined neighborhood, I heard the birds chanting their predawn melodies. Within their morning praise, I heard the answer to my prayers: "We need you, we need you, we need you." To an outsider looking out the window and enjoying a cup of coffee while listening to the morning news or getting the children ready for school, nothing extraordinary had happened: a solitary pilgrim was sauntering through the neighborhood, listening to the birds singing their morning songs. But in that moment, I received the guidance I had been seeking. Within my spirit, I heard, "Write this book."

As I continued my sunrise sojourn, this message emerged: "Let go of the book you had initially proposed and start something new. Make a fresh start. Begin again. Letting go of your previous plans will mean extra work, but if you take a new path, you will find your passion." Spiritual synchronicity struck again later that day. I picked up a text on Francis of Assisi to review what I had previously underlined, and the first passage I saw was from Francis's biographer Thomas of Celano: Francis of Assisi was "always new, always fresh, always beginning again."[2]

Unplanned moments such as these awaken us to holy adventures in which guidance appears out of nowhere and mysticism leads to mission. The divine call and the human response resound in unison. We see more deeply into reality, discover a new vocation, and begin a new way of life.

Perhaps you are looking for fresh, new ways to fulfill your vocation in your immediate community and the world. Perhaps you need to begin again, finding a way forward where there appears to be none. Pause awhile and pay attention, and you may experience God's insight coming to you in this holy moment. This book may invite you to an adventure, with God as your companion.

As I launch this text, I am grateful to my sisters and brothers who have accompanied me on this theological and spiritual journey. I give thanks for my companion of forty-five years, Kate. I am grateful for the counsel of my mentors John Cobb, David Griffin, Marie Fox, Richard Keady, and Bernard Loomer, and the wisdom of Franciscans Richard Rohr and Ilia Delio. And I give thanks for my students, colleagues, and congregants, with whom I have shared over forty years of teaching and ministry.

# CHAPTER ONE

# *Beginning Again*

I will pour out my spirit on all flesh;

your sons and your daughters shall prophesy,

your old men shall dream dreams,

and your young men shall see visions.

Even on the male and female slaves,

in those days, I will pour out my spirit.

—JOEL 2:28-29 (SEE ALSO ACTS 2:17–18)

We may discover that we are being led by God to discover the path to blessedness in the wilderness of uncertainty. A voice of out nowhere might call us to see ourselves for the first time, and as this new self-awareness unfolds, we discover God's dream for us and the path that will bring us and those around us to authentic and everlasting joy. In whatever way God's call comes, it eventually unites the inner and outer journeys, and what is private is eventually revealed in the challenges of daily life and social involvement.

I suspect that an observer would have perceived nothing extraordinary when the unkempt Francis of Assisi (1181–1226) entered the dilapidated chapel at San Damiano to pray. That observer might have heard of Francis's fall from grace and privilege. They may have remembered how Francis and his drinking companions had serenaded the young beauties of Assisi, seeking to coax them into a night of partying and romance. But now, the once-privileged Francesco ("the Frenchman"), who delighted in good food, good drink, and good companions, was alone, penniless, and ragged, without personal or spiritual resources. In outward appearance, he was a pitiful shadow of the man about town he had once been. He had left it all behind, thrown it all away, disgraced himself by leaving the family business. But hidden beneath his rags were an abundant spiritual life and a pathway to the future. His apparent poverty concealed the anticipation that the lost child would be welcomed home by his true parent; material poverty would give way to spiritual plentitude. Echoing God's call, the stones of San Damiano cried out to Francis, "Repair my church."

That same observer also might not have noticed Clare's (1194–1253) inner restlessness and desire to serve God rather than enter into an arranged marriage. They would have discounted as wishful thinking the divine words spoken to Clare's mother that her daughter would be a clear light in the world. In whatever way it comes, the call of God is always countercultural, injecting new possibilities for us and our world, and often—as in the cases of Francis and Clare —provoking negative responses and threats from friends and family.

The young theologian Bonaventure (1217–1274), while studying at the University of Paris, saw Francis's way of life as a template and inspiration for his future spiritual, intellectual, and administrative endeavors. Whether God's call is dramatic or subtle, it transforms our lives and sets us on new adventures in mysticism and mission.[3]

Francis didn't fully intuit the scope of the vocational message he received. A concrete thinker, his initial response was to gather materials and set about rebuilding the walls of the San Damiano chapel. Francis heard God's call in one place and time. Not fully sure that he had completed his divine assignment, Francis began to work on a second chapel. In the process of repairing local chapels, Francis discovered a deeper meaning in the message God had given him: "Repair the spirit of the church. It is in ruins and needs to be restored. By repairing the spirit of the church, you will repair your own life and experience the healing of purpose you need to find meaning and joy."

Scorning her culture's expectations and the prerogatives of her economic status, Clare chose the pathway of sacred simplicity and emerged as the spiritual guide of women in her time and an example for seekers in all times and places. Bonaventure discovered that theologians can join heart, mind, and hands as they experience Christ igniting the words they write.

I believe that the test of a living spirituality is to be found in its interaction with the contemporary world, whether that be the chaos and contentiousness of feudal thirteenth-century Italy or the incivility, divisiveness, and growing pluralism of twenty-first-century democracies. Lively spirituality and its theological reflections and practices must be "always new, always fresh, always beginning again" if they are to respond to the needs of a rapidly changing and often directionless world. The wisdom and traditions of the past must be integrated with God's movement toward the fresh horizons of the future.

Like Francis, we need to treasure the religious institutions that nurture us, especially the faith of our spiritual parents, while recognizing that fidelity to the insights of the past should inspire us to embody new visions for the future. Like Clare, we need to forge new paths of spirituality, grounded in fresh interpretations of the role of women as spiritual leaders. Like Bonaventure, we may be called to breathe life into our words so that theological reflection can illuminate the lively movements of God in the world. We may need to infuse the challenges of administration and institutional life with the energies of the love and the inspiration of the Holy Spirit. As God informed Francis at San Damiano, God also tells us that our world and our lives need repair and our religious communities need fresh and inspiring visions to move from apathy to empathy and hopelessness to transformation. We need to heal the soul of our church, our nation, and our planet as well as ourselves and our relationships.

### A Fresh New Morning for Spiritual Transformation

We live in a world of hope and despair, creativity and destruction. Freshness abounds and is always available to nourish us, and yet we have succumbed to brittle and lifeless visions of spirituality, society, and politics. We have pursued short-term profits and pleasures and put our planet's future in peril. Intended to be a place for spiritual transformation, a sanctuary for the marginalized and forgotten, and an inspiration for the quests of spiritual seekers, the institutional church is weary, worn out, and dispirited, out of step with a world of pluralism, pandemic, and political instability. We feel hopeless in confronting the violence that invades our schools and shopping centers, the incivility on social media, and the apathetic attitudes toward the devasting consequences of climate change.

Still, the message of Franciscan spirituality can awaken a vision of hope amid the challenges we face. A new day dawns. Spiritual adventures await us. Seeds sprout from the dark earth. Dolphins leap with joy. Fresh approaches to life's challenges emerge. We can begin again, joyfully celebrating Brother Sun and Sister Moon, and planting seeds of grace on Sister Mother Earth.

Francis, Clare, and Bonaventure would have been astounded by today's technology, but they recognized in their thirteenth-century world the same violence, apathy, alienation, and hopelessness that we experience today. Francis came to realize that the dilapidated chapel of San Damiano symbolized a broken church that had traded the lively movements of the gospel for the stagnant order, coercive power, and privileged prosperity of Constantine's Christendom. While the church shaped the empire, the empire also shaped the church, hastening the movement within the church from experience to doctrine, relationship to authority, equality to hierarchy, and simplicity to affluence. The simplicity of the wandering Savior gave way to opulence among the elite and poverty among the majority.

Francis's new vision for a community, Clare's ministry of poverty, and Bonaventure's mystical theology resemble the messages of the Baptist preachers of my childhood, particularly my father, Everett, who asserted that the good news of God's ever-fresh grace must be joined with the recognition of our current personal and planetary situation in all its wonder, beauty, ambiguity, and sin. Recognizing the concrete challenges facing the Christendom of his time was the impetus for Francis's commitment to restore the church, not only to its first-century gospel vitality but to its unique mission for his time and place.

*A Fresh Spiritual Beginning for All of Us*

Whether we are on the road embracing outcasts with Francis, cloistered with Clare serving the vulnerable who show up at our door, or studying with Bonaventure in the library or lecture hall, we who embody Franciscan spirituality hope for personal and planetary transformation. Although Francis and Clare delighted in the first-century Galilean origins of Christianity, they realized that to be faithful to Jesus, they needed to incarnate Jesus's message in their time and place. They had to share God's vision in a world characterized by violent crusades, prosperous prelates, hopeless peasants, and controversies in the church. Following the path of his spiritual ancestors, Bonaventure discovered that he needed to adapt his theological study to fresh understandings of the Franciscan tradition. He had to be a theological innovator as well as a caretaker of tradition.

In our own day, we are called to plant new gardens, restore broken churches, and renew moribund spiritualities. We can embody the fresh Pentecostal spirit of the early church to reanimate the faith of our time. With Francis, Clare, and Bonaventure, we can affirm a democracy of revelation that embraces all of humanity and overcomes the destructive impact of an "us vs. them" approach to religion and politics.

Francis, Clare, and Bonaventure inspire us to adventurous spirituality: to re-enchant and heal our spiritual practices and religious institutions and to reclaim our vocation as God's companions in healing the world. God's center is everywhere, and each moment can be a gateway to divinity. Spirit-filled and Spirit-inspired, we breathe life into the world, providing spiritual resuscitation to revive faith in the future and healing for the world.

## Fresh Franciscan Spirituality

Claiming Franciscan spirituality today requires us to embrace and transform twelfth- and thirteenth-century wisdom for the twenty-first century. Like Francis and his followers, we must join the eternal and the everchanging, the infinite and the finite. Instead of living in in a world of abstractions, we must form and transform our theology and spirituality in the world in which we live.

Francis, Clare, and Bonaventure understood the joys and challenges of the human adventure. They would have delighted in medical and scientific discoveries that promote health and reduce suffering. They would have been amazed by photos from the Hubble Space Telescope, and their images of God would have grown as they imagined a fourteen-billion-year-old, trillion-galaxy universe. They would have mourned our misuse of technology, our role in environmental destruction, and our attachment to consumerism. Racism, sexism, and marginalization of "otherness" would have inspired their prophetic challenge. The living ideas of the first Franciscans can enable us to navigate our spiritual, relational, and economic course in the twenty-first century. Not bound by the conceptual frameworks or social norms of the twelfth and thirteenth centuries or the ways of life in Assisi or Paris, their wisdom, compassion, and insight can guide us today. Faithfulness to Franciscan spirituality involves inviting other companions to join us on the journey. Francis, Clare, and Bonaventure would welcome Pierre Teilhard de Chardin, Pope Francis, Joshua Heschel, Leonardo Boff, Albert Schweitzer, Dorothy Day and many others. Dialogue with these contemporary thinkers enables us to affirm the ever-fresh spirituality of the first Franciscans and apply their insights to our time.

## Fresh Spirituality

This text is a holy adventure in what I call "theo-spirituality," the process of affirming the essential connection of theological reflection with spiritual practice. Theo-spirituality was at the heart of Bonaventure's vision joining theological and mystical experience. Theological reflection emerges from moments in which the reality of God transforms our lives. Without moments of ecstasy, transcendence, and unity, there would be no religion. Lively faith gives birth to lively religious communities. Mysticism leads to mission, and theology informs and describes spiritual experiences. Without spirituality, theology is lifeless and abstract. Apart from theology, spirituality becomes aimless and untethered to daily life. Spiritual practices become irrelevant. Faith is enriched by understanding, and understanding is enlivened by experiences of the Holy.

Franciscan spirituality invites us to start where we are in the concrete limitations of our own lives instead of reaching for some ideal and abstract world. Freshness comes in the journey and not in a prescribed destination. In walking the path with Jesus, our lives, like Francis's life, become a prayer, in which we are energized and inspired with every breath. Francis, Clare, and Bonaventure invite us to listen to our concrete joys and sorrows and then let our lives speak to the challenges of our world and our relationships.

Begin this spiritual practice with what some indigenous spiritual seekers describe as "crying for a vision." Pray for guidance to experience God's path for your life. Gaze upon Christ and be open to his guidance. Pray for the patience to listen and respond to God's call within the events of your life. Then listen to the voice of God in nature, synchronous encounters, personal intuitions, and spiritual visions. What we hear may not be clear and obvious, but it will enable us to go forward one step at a time.

Breathe deeply God's presence; let it fill your cells and your soul, illuminating body and spirit. Let your visions lead you to mission, whether in your family, community, church, or the world.

**FRESH PRAYER**

Loving Creator, give me wisdom for the living of these days.

Help me to maintain hope for the future.

In listening, let me find a path forward

where I perceive no way ahead.

Let me find guidance in companionship

with Francis, Clare, and Bonaventure.

Let me see your face in all creation,

especially in the least of those

in the human and nonhuman worlds.

Let my listening inspire action to repair

my community, church, and world.

In the name of the Healer Jesus.

Amen.

# CHAPTER TWO

# *The Ever-New God*

I am about to do a new thing;

now it springs forth; do you not perceive it?

I will make a way in the wilderness

and rivers in the desert.

—Isaiah 43:19

O most Noble Queen,

Gaze upon Christ,

Consider Christ,

Contemplate Christ,

As you desire to imitate Christ.

—Clare of Assisi

Our firmly held images of God's character and relationship to us shape our values, politics, ethics, relationships with people of other religions, and care for the earth. Our images of God may be a matter of life and death for people in despair and a planet in crisis. They may inspire us to make peace and offer hospitality to strangers or to launch crusades against political and religious opponents and commit violence against immigrants and those whose beliefs differ from our own.

If Christian faith is to be meaningful to twenty-first-century individuals and play a positive role in healing the earth and its peoples, Christians must choose the way of loving relatedness and not the path of coercive power. We must imitate the humility of God, described by Francis of Assisi, and not the arrogance of Caesar too often used by political and religious leaders. Although Francis, Clare, and Bonaventure grew up in a world of strictly defined hierarchies related to God, ecclesiastical and political decision-making, and family life, they proclaimed an alternative vision of God and the world, in which God's love invited people to cherish warm and affirmative relationships among all people as well as between humankind and the nonhuman world. Order and law, whether ecclesiastical or political, are gifts of God and need to be honored, but we also need to recognize that their purpose is to serve humanity, not control it.

Francis defied the culturally sanctioned hierarchies of his time when he abandoned his place in his family and in the social order to pursue God through holy poverty. Clare's decision to enter cloistered life challenged the wishes of the men in her family and the social norms that required her to find a socially and economically suitable mate. Later, Clare challenged a male-dominated church hierarchy when she insisted on writing a rule for her community that held to absolute poverty. She recognized that fidelity to God, reflected in agency and freedom, was as important as the standard practices of the church's hierarchy.

The first followers of Francis and Clare were known for the affirmation "God and all things." Their spiritual counsel and relationships portrayed God as lovingly involved in the world, joyfully bringing forth the diversity of flora, fauna, and humankind. They believed that God loved the world, inspiring all creation to praise. Creation was a blessing, and the path to God was through the world of embodiment and delight in the senses and not in negating the beauty and wonder of embodied, holistic existence.

Francis, Clare, and Bonaventure believed that God was relational, incarnational, and companionable. You could gaze upon God, as Clare counseled, and see God suffering on the cross and feel your own pain and joy, and the pain and joy of the human and nonhuman world. You could feel God's own pain at the suffering of all creation, human and nonhuman. More than that, the first Franciscans believed that God was in the world, actively shaping human experience, and inspiring birds' songs and wolves' howls. Francis's stigmata reflected the interplay of divine and human empathy and revealed the intimacy of a suffering

God who invites us to share in his sacrificial love, transforming self-interest into selflessness, to incarnate God's realm "on earth as it is in heaven."

"God and all things" can be described as a theological inspiration for what today is described as *panentheism*, which affirms "God in all things and all things in God." In this concept, we encounter a fresh, albeit ancient, vision of God, whose love embraces sparrows, the lilies of the field, and wayward humanity. God is the fellow sufferer who understands and the joyful companion who celebrates. The cruciform God, gazed upon by Clare, is our closest companion, experiencing our pain from the inside and inspiring us to alleviate the suffering of others. Seeking to provide a theological undergirding for the insights of Francis and Clare, Bonaventure illuminated the spirit of panentheism and divine suffering by describing God as "the One whose center is everywhere and whose circumference is nowhere."[4] In many ways, Bonaventure's brief affirmation presents a complete theology in miniature and inspires a mysticism of relatedness in which God is an infinite fountain flowing into each and every finite thing.

First, God is "the One whose center is everywhere." God is present everywhere, luring us toward wholeness. All things are touched by God. God is present in our cells and in our souls. You are the center of God's love and so is everything else. You are loved by God and so is everyone else. God centers you and God centers all creation. Within each moment of experience, God is moving, inspiring, urging, comforting, challenging, and illuminating. God delights in birds' songs and inspires their joyous melodies. Divine creativity gives birth to worms and grasshoppers and krill and kangaroos. God rejoices in the songs of humpback whales and the chanting of monks.

God's love for the world is reflected in Bonaventure's assertion that God is "within all things, but not enclosed; outside all things, but not excluded; above all things, but not aloof; below all things, but not debased."[5]

We find evidence of this idea throughout Scripture. Awestruck by divine radiance, the prophet Isaiah hears the angels singing "the whole earth is full of God's glory" (Isaiah 6:3b). The author of Psalm 148 describes each creature praising God, and God inspiring praise within each creature.

> Praise the Lord!
> Praise the Lord from the heavens;
> praise him in the heights!
> Praise him, all his angels;
> praise him, all his host!
> Praise him, sun and moon;
> praise him, all you shining stars!
> Praise him, you highest heavens

and you waters above the heavens!
Let them praise the name of the Lord,
 for he commanded and they were created.
He established them forever and ever;
he fixed their bounds, which cannot be passed.
Praise the Lord from the earth,
you sea monsters and all deeps,
fire and hail, snow and frost,
stormy wind fulfilling his command!
Mountains and all hills,
fruit trees and all cedars!
Wild animals and all cattle,
creeping things and flying birds!
Kings of the earth and all peoples,
princes and all rulers of the earth!
Young men and women alike,
old and young together! (Psalm 148:1–12)

The Psalms conclude with God's invitation to all creatures to join in a joyful democracy of praise: "Let everything that breathes praise the Lord!" (Psalm 150:6a). Our praise reflects God's praise within us. God is not on the outside looking in. God is the breath of life and fiery energy within all creation, propelling all creatures forward to claim their vocation in the cosmic adventure. God's breath gives life to us, and the Holy Spirit blows through all creation.

Reflecting the radical amazement of the psalmist, Francis's "Canticle of the Creatures" describes God's voice echoing throughout creation:

Be praised, my Lord,¹ through all your creatures,
especially through my lord Brother Sun,
who brings the day; and you give light through him.
And he is beautiful and radiant in all his splendor!
Of you, Most High, he bears the likeness.
Praised be You, my Lord, through Sister Moon
and the stars, in heaven you formed them
clear and precious and beautiful.
Praised be You, my Lord, through Brother Wind,
and through the air, cloudy and serene,
and every kind of weather through which
You give sustenance to Your creatures.
Praised be You, my Lord, through Sister Water,
which is very useful and humble and precious and chaste.
Praised be You, my Lord, through Brother Fire,
through whom you light the night and he is beautiful
and playful and robust and strong.
Praised be You, my Lord, through Sister Mother Earth,
who sustains us and governs us and who produces
varied fruits with colored flowers and herbs.

God is alive and active in all creation. God's voice echoes in all creation. This is the spiritual meaning of the doctrine of divine omnipresence. The Living God is present in new and creative ways, urging the world toward beauty and fruitfulness. Francis would have been comfortable with the evolutionary mysticism of Teilhard de Chardin, who believed that within all things dwelt the inner fire of God, aiming the creation and each creature toward the Omega Point, the realm of *shalom* in which the lion lies down with the lamb, and the once-violent wolf of Gubbio frolics with young children in the village.

God is the source of both order and novelty. God's faithfulness is found in divine creative companionship and revealed in a lively and personal relationship with all creation and every creature. God's care for us is concrete and intimate. God's presence is invitational rather than domineering, evocative rather than demanding.

Francis's mystical experience at San Damiano reflected the call and response that characterizes every moment of our lives. When he heard the words "Repair my church," Francis was experiencing the still, small voice of God, speaking from deep to deep, and Spirit to spirit, evoking Francis' highest aspirations. Francis's response was an affirmation of the grace that called him to transformation and reflection and inspired him to act. Francis's ability to align his vision with God's vision, to embody God's vision in his time and place, reflected God's Spirit challenging him to join mysticism with mission. In his quest to discern his vocation, Francis discovered that he was at the center of God's love and that God had a vision for his life. God's vision for Francis was as concrete as the walls of San Damiano. Francis's own tattered life needed repair, and in repairing the dilapidated chapel, Francis experienced his own personal healing. He found his calling as a fool for God and a lover of all creation. He also came to believe that God had an intimate vision for every created thing, and that we are obligated to honor and support God's diverse handiwork.

While Clare's experience was less dramatic, her spiritual growth reflected a persistent and ongoing movement to choose a life of loving service and companionship with God instead of an arranged marriage designed to acquire property and wealth. Clare's own journey from privilege to participation in God's mission embodies God's intimate guidance within her life. God's messages were directed to Clare, in her wealth and beauty, to become a clear spirit illuminating the world.

This same divine call centers all creation, moment by moment, and life by life. Creatures sing in unison with God, fulfilling God's vision for their lives on land, sea, and air. God's creative power in the world is invitational, not coercive. We can say no to God or embody God's call in our own unique way. Neither our negativity nor our digressions nullify God's loving care. God continues to invite us toward fulfillment through service and compassion, regardless of our responses. As Bonaventure notes, "God's power is God's humility; God's strength is God's weakness; God's greatness is God's lowliness."[6]

God's "circumference is nowhere," asserts Bonaventure. God's love is creative, and it is also receptive, including all things in God's experience. In many ways, God's loving receptivity and experience of our feelings is as important as God's wise creativity. Everything dwells within God's loving heart. Bonaventure notes, "I know myself better in God than in myself."[7] This relational understanding of divine omnipotence differs from traditional theistic and pantheistic understandings of God's experience of the world. Traditional theism describes God as outside the universe, perfect and complete, unaffected by the tragic beauty, the joy and sorrow, of history. God is the unmoved mover, emotionally distant from the tumult of creation. God knows the world from the outside. When the distant God enters the world, God's arrival is also from the outside, supernaturally moving to set things right, answering some prayers rather than others, and changing the course of history by suspending the predictable causal relationships of the natural world. Pantheism, on the other hand, affirms that God and the world are one reality, seamlessly woven together. As the saying goes, the universe, "is what it is," and nothing more. God's experience is reduced to creaturely experience, and nothing more. God is the world, and the world is God. God is not a center of love and emotion, but the world's process of evolving, living, and dying. Similar in spirit to the forceful and all-determining God of traditional theism, pantheism affirms that the current state of affairs is divinely ordained and need not be altered to ensure a more equitable world for those who experience injustice and marginalization. God is everything and everything is God, perfectly unfolding despite suffering and injustice.

In contrast to both of these theologies, a Franciscan spirituality of panentheism affirms that God is present within the world, inspiring all things to loving praise and joyful creativity. God also is the companion who embraces all things in God's loving spirit. God feels us from the inside, but God is more than our experience and creativity. In the spirit of holistic, mind-body medicine, God is the mind or spirit present everywhere within the body, touched by the body, influenced by the body. Yet God is also the spiritual guide, who directs the body's movements, initiating the moral and spiritual arcs of history that flow in and through creation as a whole and within each creature personally. God creates, but more surprisingly, God receives and responds. God's heart was touched by Francis's quest for authentic life. God felt Francis's dissatisfaction with his present life, his ambivalence about the future, and his alienation from his father. God also felt Francis's father's disappointment in his son's failure to follow in his footsteps, and his mother's anxiety at losing her son to a life of poverty. God experienced Francis's fear of people with leprosy, and inspired him to embrace a person with leprosy whom he met in his travels, and later to live with and care for those diagnosed with leprosy and separated from society.

God hears the cries of the poor, the anguish of parents whose children are victims of gun violence, and the anger of those who have been marginalized and oppressed and whose history has been hidden by people of privilege and power. God also delights in the singing of sparrows in the early morning and the flashing of fireflies on a summer evening. God feels the pain of an injured baby bird, fallen out of its nest, and the loneliness of a pet mourning the death of its human companion.

God's experience of the world is cruciform in nature. The cross is more than an event on Calvary's hill. The cross reveals God's embeddedness in all creation, sharing our joys and sorrows. When Jesus wept over Jerusalem, he was crying God's tears. When Jesus died on the cross, his pain was real, and so was God's. God feels the anguish of those who have been abandoned and persecuted. More than that, God felt the pain of the nails that pierced Jesus's body and the lashes administered by the Roman authorities. God mourned the diabolical decisions of religious and political leaders that led to Jesus's crucifixion.

The stigmata Francis received in his final years revealed God's pain within his pain. The stigmata reflected God's empathy expanding Francis's own empathy and circle of love to include all creation. Francis's God is not aloof or apathetic. God is embedded in the pain and joy of the world. Our calling, as Francis and Clare discovered, is to identify the pain of the least of these—the worm crushed by an errant footstep, the soldier wounded in battle, the leper scorned on the road—as God's pain. God experiences the pain and joy of creatures, which touch the heart of our immanent and intimate God. As Bonaventure writes, God is "totally submerged in the waters from the sole of the foot to the top of the head…. [God] appeared to you as your beloved cut through with wound upon wound in order to heal you."[8]

Gazing on the cross, as Clare counseled the royal Agnes of Prague, is not an abstract intellectual exercise, but a personal identification with God's pain on the cross and in every moment of human misery. Clare's gazing upon Jesus inspired her own solidarity with the pain of the world, and the divine and human empathy toward those who suffer also encompasses the joy of experiencing Christ's resurrection, God's loving triumph that brings healing to all creation and invites us to be messengers of hope to those who have been crushed by suffering and injustice.

## Fresh Spirituality

Our images of God truly matter. They can be a matter of life and death, of justice and injustice.

They can inspire withdrawal from the world and passive waiting for a divine rescue operation, or a commitment to embodying God's realm of *shalom*, "on earth as it is in heaven," through acts of personal kindness, earth care, and social justice.

*Imaging God*

In this first spiritual exercise, we will explore your images of God, now and throughout your life. Begin with a few moments of silence, breathing deeply the breath of God, God's Spirit, "in whom we live and move and have our being" (Acts 17:28a). Then reflect on your childhood images of God. How did you visualize God? Did you have any pictures of God? How did the adults around you describe God?

Fast-forward to your teenage and college years. Was God meaningful to you? What was your image of God when you were a teenager and young adult?

Now consider your adult images of God. What is your current image of God? Do you see God in terms of gender, male or female, or beyond gender, or in terms of wise and creative energy? What is God's relationship to the world? How does God relate to suffering and evil?

Does God have an impact on your life? Do you have an impact on God? Do your images of God shape your personal behavior, citizenship, and relationships with others?

Conclude with a time of silence and gratitude for the opportunity to explore the meaning of God's presence in your life and decision-making.

*Opening to God*

In this second spiritual practice, reflect on the Franciscan affirmation "God and all things." As you begin your day, make a commitment to attend to God's presence throughout the day. Whether eating or working, talking with a friend or family member, walking or driving, watching television or interacting on social media, train your attention to God's presence.

When you become distracted, bring yourself back to your intention by taking a deep breath and repeating "God and all things." Pay attention to the God-moments of your life, those events in which God seems more present than at other times. In these God-moments, deeply open to the messages you may be receiving from God's Spirit moving through your spirit. Align yourself, with divine humility, to the moral and spiritual arcs of God as they flow through your life to those around you.

*Something Beautiful for God*

Franciscan spirituality is relational. We are constantly shaping the lives of others by our decisions and commitments. God and others are constantly influencing the quality of our own lives. We make a difference to God and God makes a difference to us, providing guidance, insight, and inspiration in every moment.

God's presence is inspirational and invitational. Accordingly, in the Franciscan spirit, God's initiative supports and expands our own personal agency. God wants to be as free and creative as possible in terms of our impact on those around us. We are, as St. Teresa of Avila counsels, the hands, feet, and heart of God.

We can, as St. Teresa of Calcutta asserts, "do something beautiful for God."

Throughout the day, in your conversations, interactions, and digital communications, make a commitment to add beauty to the universe. Make a commitment to add beauty to God's life and the lives of all creatures.

**FRESH PRAYER**

Heart of the Universe,

thank you for the wonder of creation

and the wonder of my own life.

Help me to pay attention to the world in which I live.

Help me to share the wonders of life

in words of gratitude and acts of kindness.

Help me to see beauty everywhere

and be the embodiment of beauty,

bringing beauty and healing to every situation.

Let my heart beat with your heart,

feeling your joy and pain,

and companioning with you in healing the world.

In Jesus's name.

Amen.

# CHAPTER THREE

# Taking a Fresh Path with Jesus

If you wish to be perfect, go, sell your possessions, and
give the money to the poor, and you will have treasure in
heaven; then come, follow me.

—MATTHEW 19:21

Place your mind before the mirror of eternity!
Place your soul in the brilliance of glory!
Place your heart in the figure of divine substance.
And transform your whole being into the image of the
Godhead Itself through contemplation.

—CLARE OF ASSISI[9]

During my childhood, my parents and their peers held up
Albert Schweitzer (1875–1965) as the model of what it means
to follow Jesus. Intellectually precocious and the son of a pastor,
Schweitzer received advanced degrees in philosophy, theology,
organ, and tropical medicine. To the astonishment of many of his

colleagues in music, medicine, and theology, at thirty, Schweizer left a life of intellectual stimulation and economic privilege when he received God's call to be Christ's partner in healing the sick at a mission outpost in Lambaréné in French Equatorial Africa, today's Gabon.

Schweitzer's New Testament studies led him to embody the faith of Jesus. Although Schweitzer questioned traditional theological understandings of Jesus, he faithfully lived out the message of the One who said, "Follow me." In his encounter with the gospel portrait of Jesus, the young scholar felt called to be "a simple human being, doing something small in the spirit of Jesus."[10] Schweitzer discovered that we can know Jesus by walking the path of Jesus, faithfully following the Savior's call in our daily lives, whether in the classroom or in the mission field. When asked why he left the academic world to treat the sick of central Africa, he responded simply, "Because my master asked me."[11] Schweitzer has been compared to Francis of Assisi in that both men left the promises of privilege, property, and profession to follow Jesus. Both affirmed reverence for life and the value and beauty of the nonhuman world as essential to the Christian vision. Schweitzer concluded his epoch-making study of the quest to discover the authentic Jesus of history with words that describe the pilgrim saint of Assisi as well as himself, the medical mystic of Africa.

He comes to us as One unknown, without a name, as of
old, by the lakeside, He came to those men who knew Him
not. He speaks to us the same words: "Follow thou me!"
and sets us to the tasks which He has to fulfill for our time.
He commands. And to those who obey Him, whether they
be wise or simple, He will reveal himself in the toils, the
conflicts, the sufferings which they shall pass through in
His fellowship, and, as an ineffable mystery, they shall learn
in their own experience Who He is.[12]

Our childhood and youthful values often shape our spiritual
destinies. As a child, Albert Schweitzer was sensitive to the pain
of the nonhuman world. He refused to hunt and experienced
deep sorrow when an aging horse was to be slaughtered for meat
byproducts. Later, Schweitzer formulated an ethical system based
on "reverence for life." In similar fashion, seven hundred years
earlier, the courtly Francis was known for his generous spirit.
Anyone in need could count on his support, and he always had
a coin in his pocket for a beggar or a needy family. After Francis
encountered the living Christ, his circle of generosity included
all creation, human and nonhuman, and his quest for poverty
was motivated by the gospel vision of spiritual solidarity with
the world.

Worried about her first pregnancy, Clare Offreduccio's mother
heard God's voice addressing her anxieties: "Don't be afraid,

for you will joyfully bring forth a clear light that will illumine the world." Clare's own clarity of spirit was awakened when she heard Francis's message of finding God by following Jesus's path of simplicity and solidarity. Together, these two spiritual companions illuminated the Christianity of their time and inspired others to follow Jesus in compassionate and humble service, giving up the world of power and privilege to heal their souls and the soul of the planet. Although Francis and Clare grew up in a social order in which status determined whether a person traveled by horse, carriage, or on foot, these spiritual pilgrims recognized that Jesus can be found only in the walking, both literally and figuratively. Francis and Clare discovered the living Christ by following in his footsteps, living in the style of Jesus, welcoming the outcast, embracing the lost, and putting God's realm above all else. Francis was always on the move, always discovering fresh spiritual vistas and encountering new horizons. Clare spent most of her life in a physically cloistered but open-spirited monastery. Though rooted in one place, Clare's spirit was cosmopolitan and hospitable to the villagers of Assisi, a mile up the hill, as well as to spiritual pilgrims and those in need of medical care.

While religious doctrines set boundaries and give guidelines for faithful living, a living faith is experiential and ethical, charting a pathway in the footprints of Jesus. Although Francis and Clare used the word *Christ* to describe God's Beloved Child, their day-to-day faith was formed by gospel accounts of the life and teachings of the embodied Christ, the first-century Galilean, Jesus of Nazareth, along with the cosmic and transcendent preexisting Logos-Christ described in John 1:1-18. In the spirit of 1 Corinthians 13, Francis and Clare knew that if we "understand all mysteries and all knowledge," grounded in the doctrines of the church, we are nothing if we lack the love of Jesus embodied in our daily lives. The test of orthodoxy is not found in adherence to doctrinal purity or inflexible ethical absolutes, often enforced coercively on others, but in the interplay of mysticism, mission, and morality.

The fruit of orthodoxy is orthopraxy, a commitment to embodying the gospel lifestyle of Jesus of Nazareth. One of the great tragedies of Christian history can be found in the church's creation of creeds and doctrines which separate belief from action and theology from morality. As significant as they were in the formation of the Christian tradition, the Apostles' Creed and the Nicene Creed focus primarily on metaphysics of faith and the nature of God, Christ, and the Holy Spirit but say nothing about the ethics and lifestyle of Jesus. A person can boldly claim to be an orthodox Christian, affirming the creeds of the church and the authority of Scripture, yet follow business and political practices that disregard planetary well-being, economic justice, human rights, democratic institutions, and concern for strangers and immigrants—the very creation that Jesus came to heal and save.

The fresh spirituality of Francis was grounded in a series of encounters with God in which faith and action were joined in the call to be Jesus's companion in repairing the church and healing the world. Following a time of convalescence, the youthful Francis "prayed with all his heart that the Eternal and True God guide his way and *teach him to do his will.*"[13] Initially, he assumed that he would be serving God as a soldier and nobleman, until once more he experienced the voice of God speaking directly to him, "Francis, who can do more for you, a lord or his servant, a rich man or a beggar?" When he replied a lord or a rich man could do more, he was asked, "Then why are you abandoning the Lord to devote yourself to a servant? Why are you choosing a beggar instead of God, who is infinitely rich?" Francis queried, "Lord, what will you have me do?" The divine voice responded, "Go back to your hometown. The vision which you saw foretold a spiritual achievement which will be accomplished in you by God's will, not man's [*sic*]."[14]

Shortly thereafter, after hearing the assigned gospel reading at Mass, Francis asked the priest to explain the meaning of Jesus's path of simplicity. When he heard that Christ's disciples *should not possess gold or silver or money, or carry on their journey a wallet or sack or bread or a staff, nor have shoes or two tunics, but that they should preach the kingdom of God and penance,* the holy Francis immediately *exulted in the Spirit of God.* "This is what I want," he said, "this is what I seek, this is what I desire with all my heart."[15]

Filled with joy, Francis put down his staff, gave away his second tunic, and exchanged his leather belt for a cord. From that moment on, Francis knew that the gospel was to be found primarily in fidelity to Christ's way of life and secondarily in doctrines about the Savior.

While Francis critically reflected on his mystical experiences, counting the cost of discipleship, and often reached out to spiritual companions such as Clare for counsel, Francis also believed in divine synchronicity—that God would give him the guidance he needed at the right time and by the right means, whether through a Scripture passage, visionary experience, divine voice, companion's counsel, or serendipitous encounter. Divine wisdom is everywhere, and when we attend to God's vision, rather than our own willfulness, we will find our way through the complexities of life. Bonaventure noted that Francis joined thought and action to illumine his spiritual adventures: "He read continually the sacred books, and what had once entered his mind he retained firmly in his memory."[16]

An early collection of stories about Francis and his followers, *The Little Flowers of St. Francis*, gives a more detailed account of God's revelation to Francis through the words of Scripture. Traveling with one of his first disciples, Bernard of Quintavalle, Francis asked the priest who had celebrated Mass to prayerfully open the missal to three texts to give the two pilgrims guidance for their spiritual journey. After making the sign of the cross over the missal, the priest was directed to the first text: "If you wish to be perfect, go, sell your possessions, and give the money to the poor, and you will have treasure in heaven; then come, follow me" (Matthew 19:21). The priest was guided to a second verse, "Take nothing for your journey, no staff, nor bag, nor bread, nor money—not even an extra tunic" (Luke 9:3). The priest prayerfully opened the missal a third time, and read Jesus's command to his disciples, "If any want to become my followers, let them deny themselves and take up their cross and follow me" (Mark 8:34b). Francis and Bernard received practical guidance from Scripture that joined head, heart, and hands. Spiritually enlightened by their encounter with Scripture, Francis instructed Bernard, "This is the wisdom that Jesus Christ has given to us. You should do exactly as you have heard. And thanks to God for showing us the true way of life."[17] Francis knew that spirituality involved the whole person. Mysticism leads to mission and spirituality inspires service. Doctrine and spiritual experience are lifeless apart from works of loving sacrifice.

Like that of her spiritual companion, Clare's life was an ongoing revelation of the prophetic words given to her mother, fulfilling her vocation as a "clear light that would illumine the world." From childhood, Clare embodied the Christ-like graces of humility, simplicity, and hospitality. She sought abundant life in prayer and solitude, and in relationship with Jesus. Her life was one of ongoing gazing, contemplating, and imitating the life of Christ. Clare found a pathway to following Jesus initially in hearing the words of Francis and then engaging in spiritual direction with him. Twelve years her senior, he was first her mentor and later her friend and spiritual companion. Francis showed her the way of Jesus, and in return, Clare gave Francis counsel when he sought direction for his own spiritual path, such as whether he should be a hermit or a pilgrim and itinerant preacher in the way of Christ.

### Francis, Clare, and the Way of Jesus

Francis was inspired by the life of Jesus. His goal was to become, in the words of another reformer, Martin Luther, a "little Christ." Francis sought to embody the lifestyle of Jesus and to be fully congruent with the Savior in thought, word, and deed. Both Francis and Clare saw the cross as decisive in Christ's life, an inspiration for them to take up their own crosses in sacrificial living. The cross of Christ itself was a reflection—in fact, the culmination—of Jesus's earthly ministry, the most dramatic example of the way of Jesus, the friend of sinners, healer, movement leader, and wisdom teacher.[18] The cross was the ultimate manifestation of Jesus's sacrificial living and commitment to put God before everything else, including life itself.

Jesus's life was cruciform from the moment he claimed his ministry, following his baptism by John the Baptist. Every action of Jesus reflected his willingness to follow God's vision, to be the incarnation of God's love, even when his obedience to God's vision led to persecution and the cross. Francis and Clare sought to embody the apostle Paul's description of Jesus Christ in their own evangelical piety:

> Let the same mind be in you that was in Christ Jesus, who,
> though he existed in the form of God,
> did not regard equality with God
> as something to be exploited,
> but emptied himself,
> taking the form of a slave,
> being born in human likeness.
> And being found in human form,
>  he humbled himself
> and became obedient to the point of death—
> even death on a cross. (Philippians 2:5–8)

In their spiritual adventures, Francis and Clare both sought to live in accordance with the mind of Christ, attuning every movement and choice to the sacrificial path of Jesus. They not only asked, "What would Jesus do?" but they also asked, "How would Jesus live?" and "Whom would Jesus love?"

Clare's advice to Agnes of Prague, a Bohemian princess who, like Clare, opted for a monastic life of simplicity and service, reflects the holistic, embodied spirit of Franciscan spirituality.

Consider Christ,

Contemplate Christ,

As you desire to imitate Christ.[19]

The Christ Francis and Clare imitated and taught was the Christ of the gospels, the humble Galilean who sacrificed the privileges of transcendent divinity, proclaimed the good news of God's realm, and went about doing good, healing the sick, welcoming lepers, and embracing rich and poor alike. The Christ, who emptied himself of divine power and independence to be united with humanity in sacrificial love, was their model. Their imitation of Jesus was more than merely acting out Jesus's life; it was living the life of Jesus in their time and place.

At the heart of Francis's and Clare's biblical vision was the Sermon on the Mount, and most especially the Beatitudes. Just as Jesus turned the world upside down, ushering in God's new age of *shalom*, liberating captives, and proclaiming God's *shalom* (see Luke 4:18–19), Francis's message of peace and simplicity turned upside down the divisiveness and violence of twelfth-century Italy and the opulence of the Roman Catholic Church. Francis lived out the prophetic spirit of the Beatitudes, presenting an alternative vision to both church and state, as he sought to be God's companion in healing the world, beginning with the transformation of church, and expanding his mission to include healing the whole earth, Christian and non-Christian, human and nonhuman. Francis invites us to embody the Beatitudes in our time.

Blessed are the poor in spirit, for theirs is the kingdom of heaven.

Blessed are those who mourn, for they will be comforted.

Blessed are the meek, for they will inherit the earth.

Blessed are those who hunger and thirst for righteousness, for they will be filled.

Blessed are the merciful, for they will receive mercy.

Blessed are the pure in heart, for they will see God.

Blessed are the peacemakers, for they will be called children of God.

Blessed are those who are persecuted for righteousness' sake, for theirs is the kingdom of heaven.

Blessed are you when people revile you and persecute you and utter all kinds of evil against you falsely on my account.

Rejoice and be glad, for your reward is great in heaven, for in the same way they persecuted the prophets who were before you. (Matthew 5:3-12)

The Beatitudes articulate what it means to have "the mind of Christ" in the complexities and challenges of daily life. Jesus's countercultural blessings also reflect the values embodied in his table fellowship with sinners, embrace of outcasts, healing of the "unclean" sick, and willingness to take up his own cross for our salvation.

When Francis described himself as a "*jongleur* for God," a minstrel, fool, juggler, or clown for Jesus, people questioned his own set of values, if not his mental stability. How can a sane person give up a life of comfort to follow the path of poverty? How can you find joy in simplicity? How can poverty bring contentment and happiness? If everyone follows your lead and abandons family fortune, how will society survive? Yet true happiness, Francis and Clare believed, came from the no that says yes. In turning their backs on marriage, power, and possessions, and saying no to their culture's materialistic and status-oriented value system, they said yes to companionship with Jesus and the experience of eternity in the midst of time. In taking up their cross, Francis and Clare discovered that Christ was carrying it for them!

### Gazing on the Beatitudes

In the spirit of Clare's counsel, let us take a moment to contemplate more carefully the Beatitudes, Christ's countercultural blessings that were pivotal to early Franciscan spirituality. I must admit that I am not prepared to follow these blessings completely. I frankly struggle to follow them—period! Perhaps you feel as I do about their focus on the blessings of persecution, poverty, and pain. As a "retired" pastor and theologian, I take note of my retirement assets and pension plans, and I have my mortgage and utility payments debited from my checking account so I won't pay a late fee if I forget to send my payments. I want people to purchase the books I write and invite me to give lectures and seminars, and I am not looking forward to facing my own death or grieving the deaths of loved ones. I still want to be "somebody," honored by my peers, colleagues, congregants, and readers. And yet, in contrast to my prudence, the risk-taking and downwardly mobile spirit of Beatitudes undergirds the free spirits of Francis and Clare, who believed that "if you have God, you have everything."

The Beatitudes remind us of the graceful interdependence of life. They alert us to our dependence on God and God's world for our well-being, and our need to be in relationship with others to experience the fullness of life. If God is your ultimate concern then your life finds its meaning in eternity and not in the anxieties of temporality.

The Beatitudes do not devalue earthly life or our quest for *shalom* in our citizenship and political participation. They place our lives in God's care, trusting fully in the faithfulness of God who promises that if we lose our life for God's sake, we will gain peace of mind in this life and everlasting joy in the next. In trusting God, the temporal world of change and uncertainty becomes the pathway into divine companionship and eternal life. Everyday life takes on the spirit of eternity, and outcasts become angels in disguise.

The Beatitudes by which Francis and Clare lived are revolutionary and countercultural in every century and social order. Their sense of dependence on God's power subverts the power plays of potentates, politicians, and patricians. The Beatitudes challenge images of the self-made person, whose success is solely the result of their own efforts. As Francis and Clare taught, those who have much also have much to protect. Francis noted that without possessions, he had nothing to fear from robbers or misfortune. Francis's and Clare's life of solidarity with all creation, most especially outcasts, people with leprosy, and peasants, reflected their sense of graceful interdependence. Recognizing that life is a gift, and that we depend on the efforts of others—and ultimately God—for any success we have liberates us from the anxiety of reputation and reward and frees us to live joyfully, knowing that "this is the day that the Lord has made; let us rejoice and be glad in it" (Psalm 118:24).

In a time of civil conflict, similar to our own time in which tribalism subverted community, and Christians and Muslims battled one another over the holy city, Jerusalem, Francis saw himself as a blessed peacemaker, greeting everyone and beginning each sermon with the words, "The peace of the Lord be with you." Having nothing of his own, depending fully on God, Francis had no enemies. Even the feared Muslims, in a time of Crusades, were to be treated with honor and respect. Mercy, purity, and peace may lead to persecution. But, as Jesus promises, the gift of sacrificial living, of holy poverty, is experiencing God's companionship in the present moment, come what may, and living in the hope of everlasting life with God as our companion. The self-emptying Christ is exalted and glorified. Our own self-emptying opens us to the glories of the universe and life abundant even in times of strife.

### Having the Mind of Christ

A friend of mine once described the apostle Paul's counsel—"Let the same mind be in you that was in Christ Jesus"—as a Christian koan, similar in spirit to the Zen Buddhist use of countercultural or intellectually perplexing phrases as a means of liberating the spirit and facilitating enlightenment. Each day, my friend prayed, "Let me have the mind of Christ. Help me understand what it means to have Jesus's mind." Although he never claimed, and no mystic ever claims, full alignment with "the mind of Christ," over time, his daily decisions in his business and personal life became more Christlike. He experienced a greater sense of humility and solidarity with struggling humanity, as he recognized his own imperfections and inability to live Christ fully. Like Francis, his temptations called him to prayer and persistence in the pathway of Jesus. Following Francis, he discovered that his confessions of spiritual struggle enlivened his commitment to be a little Christ.

He knew, as did Francis, that confession deepens the spirit, frees us from prevarication and denial, and enables us to begin again, trusting that God will supply all our needs.

Francis patterned his life after the Sermon on the Mount, and those who seek to embody the Franciscan spirit would do well to embrace Jesus's counsel from the Sermon:

> "Therefore I tell you, do not worry about your life, what you will eat or what you will drink, or about your body, what you will wear. Is not life more than food and the body more than clothing? Look at the birds of the air: they neither sow nor reap nor gather into barns, and yet your heavenly Father feeds them. Are you not of more value than they? And can any of you by worrying can add a single hour to your span of life? And why do you worry about clothing? Consider the lilies of the field, how they grow; they neither toil nor spin, yet I tell you, even Solomon in all his glory was not clothed like one of these. But if God so clothes the grass of the field, which is alive today and tomorrow is thrown into the oven, will he not much more clothe you— you of little faith? Therefore do not worry, saying, 'What will we eat?' or 'What will we drink?' or 'What will we wear?' For it is the Gentiles who strive for all these things, and indeed your heavenly Father knows that you need all these things. But strive first for the kingdom of God and his righteousness, and all these things will be given to you as well." (Matthew 6:25–33)

Inspired by Francis and Clare, I seek to gaze at the life of Jesus and to follow in his footsteps. I have as my goal, albeit imperfectly achieved, to follow Jesus's way, to be a "little Christ," in my daily life and relationships. I want to incarnate the One who came to liberate the captives, free the oppressed, preach good news to the poor, and proclaim God's *shalom* in my citizenship and politics (see Luke 4:18–19). Yet I still remain among those who can be described as the "worried well" and "anxious affluent." I am privileged in terms of time, talent, and treasure. I benefit from generous pensions and Social Security. I live in a safe neighborhood in one of the most desirable suburban communities in the United States. I have more than enough to eat and drink. I have the leisure to travel, write, study, and spend time with my wife and our son's family. During the course of world history, few have lived as lavishly as I do today! And yet I am anxious about finances and health. I am concerned about my reputation and prestige as a teacher and writer. Despite leisure, education, and talent as a writer and teacher, I worry about meeting schedules and deadlines. I need to take seriously Jesus's counsel to "consider the lilies of the field" and "the birds of the air." I need to discern what it means to "seek first God's realm." I need to embrace Franciscan simplicity in a world of complexity and affluence.

While it is unlikely that you, my reader, and I, the writer, will sell all we have and give to the poor or abandon the prerogatives of financial security, we need the wisdom of Francis and Clare to live generously and simply, open to the glories of each new day. Following the counsel to seek first God's realm enables us to let go of our stranglehold on our time, talent, and treasure; to experience the joy of the here and now; and to embrace personally and politically our connection and responsibility to Brother Sun, Sister Moon, Sister Mother Earth, and all of this wondrous, fragile planet. A life devoted to continuous prayer, self-awareness, and compassion, even in our human imperfection, opens the door to divine abundance and the recognition that in every situation God will supply our deepest needs.

### Francis and the Parent of All Creation

Francis placed the Lord's Prayer, the Our Father, at the center of community life. Francis enjoined his followers to internalize the wisdom of Jesus's prayer by regular repetition, letting the words soak in so that they might come to define their whole lives. Francis and his companions regularly sang the Lord's Prayer. To Francis and Clare, God was fatherly, lovingly creating the world and powerfully loving the world. Listen with heart, mind, and soul to Jesus's Prayer:

> Our Father, who art in heaven,
> hallowed be thy name;
> thy kingdom come;
> thy will be done;
> on earth as it is in heaven.

Give us this day our daily bread.
And forgive us our trespasses,
as we forgive those who trespass against us.
And lead us not into temptation;
but deliver us from evil.
For thine is the kingdom,
the power and the glory,
now and forever.

Always fresh and always new, the Lord's Prayer evolves along with our growing understanding of the universe and the significance of the nonhuman world. I have found meaning in a version of the Lord's Prayer from the New Zealand Prayer Book of the Anglican Church, influenced by the earth-based spirituality of the Maori and Polynesian peoples. I believe that the poet of the Canticle of the Creatures would have delighted in this indigenous version of Jesus's prayer.

Eternal Spirit Earth-Maker, Pain-Bearer, Life-Giver, source of all that is and that shall be, Father and Mother of us all. Loving God, in whom is heaven. The hallowing of your name echoes through the universe! The way of your justice be followed by the peoples of the earth! Your heavenly will be done by all created beings! Your commonwealth of peace and freedom sustain our hope and come on earth. With the bread we need for today, feed us. In the hurts we absorb from one another, forgive us. In times of temptation and test, spare us. From the grip of all that is evil, free us. For you reign in the glory of the power that is love, now and forever. Amen.

Celtic spiritual guide and author Philip Newell has composed another version of the Lord's Prayer, reflective of the spirit of Francis: the *Casa del Sol* Prayer of Jesus.

Ground of all being.
Mother of life, Father of the universe,
Your name is sacred, beyond speaking.
May we know your presence,
May your longings be our longings
In heart and in action.
May there be food for the human family today
And for the whole earth community.
Forgive us the falseness of what we have done
As we forgive those who are untrue to us.
Do not forsake us in our time of conflict
But lead us into new beginnings.
For the light of life,
The vitality of life,
And the glory of life,
Are yours now and forever.

If sparrows and wolves can praise God in their unique ways, humans can also approach the Heart of the Universe with names that reflect their unique cultural and spiritual experiences. Following in the footprints of Jesus means living by the all-embracing spirit of the Sermon on the Mount, trusting God in times of uncertainty, transforming enemies into friends, providing bread for all our kinfolk, and recognizing God as "our" parent, not just the patriarch of a particular nation, religious tradition, or species. Those who follow the spirit of the Lord's Prayer become mystical activists seeking to incarnate God's realm "on earth as it is in heaven." Following the vision of *shalom*, in which everyone has enough bread and enemies are reconciled, moves us from apathy to empathy and passivity to empowerment, so that the whole earth will reflect God's vision. For Francis and Clare, this meant living simply and welcoming all in the spirit of Jesus. For us, following God's vision of *shalom* on earth may mean prayer and protest, activism and alternative economic values.

Francis and Clare experienced the Holy in the encounters of everyday life. What is discovered in mystical experience—direct encounters with the Living, Loving God—inspires mission outreach to heal a broken world and gives birth to day-to-day acts of hospitality, inclusion, and lovingkindness.

## Fresh Spirituality

Francis and Clare sought to live in the style of Jesus. One of the greatest theologians of Western Christianity, their companion Bonaventure, became a Franciscan out of admiration of the simplicity of their spiritual lives. Yet this erudite theologian knew, as did his spiritual parents, that prior to theological reflection is the lived experience, born out of encounters with our Living, Loving God and daily companionship with Jesus of Nazareth. More than an intellectual abstraction, the Incarnation in its concreteness reminds us that God can be found on every pathway and through every encounter. The cross invites us to sacrifice—to live simply and face adversity and controversy—to be God's companion in healing the world. The empty tomb symbolizes God's open future, the hope of everlasting life, for God's children of all times, places, cultures, races, religions, and continents. In following the spirit of the Sermon on the Mount, we discover that God calls us to be "the light of the world" and "to let our light shine" (Matthew 5:14–16).

In the following exercises, we can discover the path Jesus has set before us and realize that our vocation as his beloved children will be found in the walking.

*Praying the Our Father*

The Lord's Prayer, the Prayer of Jesus, joins mysticism, mission, and morality. Grounded in intimacy with God, living the Lord's Prayer as Francis and his followers did inspires intimacy and reconciliation with friends and enemies alike and challenges us to embody God's realm "on earth as it is in heaven."

In this spiritual practice, spend a few days prayerfully reading the three versions of Jesus's Prayer noted in this chapter. One approach involves the following:

• Set aside a time of silent prayer.

• Ask for guidance in discerning God's vision.

• Read prayerfully each version of the Lord's Prayer, with a time of silence between each version.

• Give thanks for God's ever-present and wondrously diverse guidance and inspiration.

• Open yourself to divine movements in your life through words, intuitions, dreams, and encounters.

• Let God lead you toward incarnating Jesus's prayer in your personal life and relationships.

• Give thanks for God's all-encompassing grace, companionship, and guidance.

*Lectio on the Beatitudes*

Francis and his followers encountered Scripture holistically, with heart, hands, and spirit, as well as mind. Scripture was a living text for them, intended to speak personally to each person in their unique situation, calling them to discover their calling. In this spiritual practice, we let the Beatitudes come alive through an updated and fresh approach to *lectio divina*, or holy reading, practiced initially in the Benedictine tradition.[20] Contemporary people seldom have hours to let a biblical text soak in. Given our schedules, often ten to fifteen minutes is the most time we can set aside for spiritual practices. Moreover, contemporary people want streamlined spirituality in everyday language. In many ways, this was Francis's goal as well. In our fresh approach to *lectio divina*, I invite you to:

- Take a moment of silence, breathing deeply your connection with God and the world around you.
- Take a moment for gratitude. For what are you thankful today?
- Read the Beatitudes (Matthew 5:3–12) twice, slowly and prayerfully.
- For three to five minutes, open your heart to any insights that come. Sometimes a random message is the most profound—a word, phrase, song (popular or religious), event, or image.
- Focus on your insights for a few moments, letting them sink in, as you ask God for understanding.
- Ask about its meaning for your life today and how following this insight might change your life.
- Write down a few sentences to ground the insight in your journal.
- Conclude with a prayer of thanksgiving, asking for divine guidance in embodying the insight throughout your day.
- Throughout the day, remember your insight, noting where it might illuminate your current activities.

*Being the Light of the World*

Described as the perfect Christian by Ernst Renan, and the Second Christ by Bonaventure, Francis sought to be a light in a world of chaos and upheaval, in which even the church and its leadership had lost its way. We need to see and be the light in our equally chaotic and wayward world, in which the values of Jesus are subverted and manipulated by those who claim to be the most orthodox Christians. In this practice, begin by reading Jesus's affirmation of his disciples, then and now, pondering its meaning for your life.

> "You are the light of the world. A city built on a hill cannot be hid. No one after lighting a lamp puts it under the bushel basket, but on the lampstand, and it gives light to all in the house. In the same way, let your light shine before others, so that they may see your good works and give glory to your Father in heaven." (Matthew 5:14–16)

When you have set aside fifteen minutes for stillness, find a comfortable place to sit, and breathe deeply and prayerfully, letting the breath of life connect you with all creation. As you breathe, visualize a healing and empowering light flowing in and through you, illuminating your soul and every cell of your body. Visualize this light filling you completely, bringing health and wholeness to mind, body, and spirit. As you exhale during this time of contemplation, visualize the light going forth, bringing peace and wholeness to the world.

Throughout the day, seek to be the light in your activities, encounters, and relationships. In every situation, especially those in which conflict or tension arises, look deeply at those around you, discerning and bringing forth the light within them to bring God's peace and wholeness.

**FRESH PRAYER**

Jesus, walk with me in paths of humility and simplicity.

Show me your presence in each person I meet.

Guide my steps to be of service to those I meet.

Illumine my heart that I might shine brightly,

bringing your light to the world.

Amen.

# CHAPTER FOUR

# *Growing in Wisdom and Stature*

And Jesus increased in wisdom and in years, and in divine and human favor.

—LUKE 2:52

Burning with divine love,
the blessed father Francis was always eager
to try his hand at brave deeds,
and walking in the way of God's commands
with heart wide open,
he longed to reach the summit of perfection.

—BONAVENTURE[21]

As a *jongleur* for Christ, playing the part of a fool, clown, minstrel, and raconteur, Francis enjoyed listening to, reading, and telling stories. Although he was a meditative mystic, legend has it that Francis was so loquacious that he would tell stories and give spiritual counsel to swallows, larks, fish, rabbits, and wolves. Although he spoke in the vernacular, more interested in communicating than in showing off his intelligence with complicated theological puzzles, Francis was, according to Bonaventure, a serious student of Scripture and spiritual literature. As he sought to imitate Jesus, no doubt he saw great similarities between his life and the gospel stories. He patterned his behavior after the one whose life he sought to imitate. I believe that he likely saw himself in the story of young Jesus in the Temple.

According to Luke's gospel, each year Jesus's family, along with many of their friends from Nazareth, sojourned to Jerusalem to celebrate the Passover and recall the stories of the Israelites' liberation from servitude in Egypt. When it was time to return to Jerusalem, his parents retraced their steps to Nazareth. Along the way, they discovered that the twelve-year-old Jesus, on the verge of adulthood in the Jewish tradition, was not with the party returning home. Perhaps, they thought, he was traveling with friends, playing and telling stories, and enjoying independence from parental supervision. They scoured the caravan of pilgrims and, unable to find Jesus, returned to the Temple, where they found their son engaged in lively theological conversations with the priests and teachers, listening and asking questions. Upset with their son's irresponsible behavior, Mary queried, "Child, why have you treated us like this? Your father and I have been anxiously looking for you." To which Jesus, in a bit of polite adolescent rebellion, responded, "Why were you searching for me? Did you not know that I must be in my Father's house?"

Like so many parents of preteens and teenagers, then and now, Mary and Joseph did not understand him!

The story of Jesus in the Temple ends with the affirmation, "And Jesus increased in wisdom and in years, and in divine and human favor" (Luke 2:52). While this translation prefers "years" as a more accurate rendering of the Greek, I believe that the traditional use of the word "stature" more truly describes Jesus's spiritual development. Many people, even those of influence such as billionaires, celebrities, and politicians, grow in years with little apparent emotional and spiritual growth. Growing in stature, expansiveness, and transformation is what matters. Becoming a larger-souled person or, in the aspirations of Francis, longing "to reach the summit of perfection" is the goal of the spiritual journey.

Francis likely appreciated Jesus's rebellious streak and his countercultural decision to place his relationship with God ahead of family in a culture where family mattered above everything else. Francis may have seen himself in Jesus's distancing himself from his parents' values: Francis was a spiritually rebellious youth who defied his father to follow the way of Jesus. He knew his father couldn't understand how a child of privilege would throw away his life with the same carelessness as he had discarded his clothing for a life of naked poverty. Family matters, so his father asserted, even more than following God. In turning his back on his family, Francis had traded his good name, family identity, and legacy for an uncertain future. Reflecting on his own spiritual journey with Jesus's countercultural mission as his model, perhaps, Francis may have remembered the words of the apostle Paul: "Do not be conformed to this world, but be transformed by the renewing of your minds, so that you may discern what is the will of God—what is good and acceptable and perfect" (Romans 12:2).

In turning his back on materialism, prestige, marriage, and involvement in the violence promoted by warring villages and sanctioned by the church, Francis embraced a life of constant spiritual transformation. From now on, he would be "always new, always fresh, always beginning again." He would be committed to growing in wisdom and stature and expanding his circle of compassion and concern. He left behind Assisi's mercantile parochialism to embrace spiritual cosmopolitanism—to become a citizen of God's world.

One of my theological mentors, Bernard Loomer, believed that the evocation of spiritual size and stature is at the heart of the spiritual adventure and essential to mature faith. Loomer asserted that if a religious institution or belief system is small—that is, cramped intellectually and relationally—it should be discarded as irrelevant and injurious to individuals and communities.

> By size I mean the stature of a person's soul, the range and depth of his love, his capacity for relationships. I mean the volume of life you can take into your being and still

maintain your integrity and individuality, the intensity and variety of outlook you can entertain in the unity of your being without feeling defensive or insecure. I mean the strength of your spirit to encourage others to become freer in the development of their diversity and uniqueness.[22]

Francis and Clare had big spirits, able to embrace the depth and breadth of human experience, and able to find God in all things and all things in God. Francis's and Clare's lives were an ongoing adventure in growing in wisdom and stature. The beautiful, intelligent, and sought-after Clare gave up a life of comfort and wealth for an intimate relationship with Jesus as her companion, guide, and pattern. Recognizing the image of God in herself, Clare claimed spiritual equality with her male peers and proclaimed her ability to chart the course of her community. Francis grew from a partying youth into an unintentionally rebellious ascetic, prayerful church contractor and healer, cosmopolitan spiritual guide, and companion to the nonhuman world. Their lives serve as a pattern for our own twenty-first-century commitment to a spirituality of stature, a countercultural spirituality transformed by constant renewal in relationship to God.

### From Self-Interest to God Interest

"The arc of the moral universe is long, but it bends toward justice." This quote, popularized by Martin Luther King Jr. and

Barack Obama, comes from a speech by the nineteenth-century abolitionist Unitarian pastor Theodore Parker. While Parker confessed that we can never claim to fully discern the moral arc's destination—to do so would be to claim to know fully the mind of God!—this arc moves through our lives, communities, and planetary history. An equally inspirational spiritual arc that moves through our lives and history inspires us to transcend self-interest in favor of global community and world loyalty.

Francis and Clare were attentive to God's moral and spiritual arcs in their lives and missions. Their lives followed a pattern of moving from privilege to compassion, wealth to simplicity, focus on self to focus on others, and local prejudice to global hospitality. Francis and Clare chose simplicity and holy poverty to prune away distractions from their One True Love and embrace solidarity with the marginalized and outcast. Their choice of simplicity and downward mobility reflected their commitment to spiritual growth and not a turning from the world.

In the world loyalty characteristic of Franciscan spirituality, there is no "other"; we are all one in our divine origins and destiny. Clare and Francis sacrificed the narrow, cramped, self-interested ego, always on the defensive, always envious of others' successes, for the mind of Christ, all-embracing in hospitality, compassion, and stature. Their cosmopolitan spirituality challenges us to grow beyond the narrow confines of race, gender, nation, and species, in the quest to become kin with all creation.

### From Inferior to Blessed

While women in the twelfth and thirteen centuries were the objects of courtly love and romantic poetry, they were also seen as the spiritual and intellectual inferiors of men. Their vocation was hearth, home, and childbearing among the peasants and middle classes, and, beyond that, the opportunity for social advancement and the birth of a male heir to carry on the name among the wealthy. Women were typically defined by the values and needs of their fathers and husbands.

Clare was intelligent and beautiful, but, according to the norms of Italian society, the best she could hope for would be to make a good marriage that would bring wealth and prestige to her family. She might exert power as the lady of the house, attended by servants responding to her every whim, but she would have no place in society other than as a nobleman's wife.

Even after she entered the Franciscan community, Clare's cloistered life was both a choice and a necessity. As a twelfth-century woman, her movements were circumscribed in contrast to the more active spiritualities available to men. Despite her spiritual advancement, she could not escape the religious judgment that described women as "occasions of sin," tempting religious seekers and monks from the pathway of celibacy and obedience. In describing the spiritual status of women, Franciscan scholar Ilia Delio states that, "women were seen as a source of sin, as secondary images of God." Women's souls were judged deficient in comparison to their male counterparts in society and in the church, "defined through their bodies alone, they were not capable of being an image of God."[23]

Embracing her full humanity and challenging her culture and faith tradition, albeit gently and with nuance, Clare recognized her spiritual stature and spiritual equality with her male counterparts. Although she described herself as Francis's "little plant," Clare grew in spiritual stature in her relationship to Francis, from a student and admirer, to a spiritual leader, to a wise counselor who advised Francis, and ultimately to a spiritual companion and equal. In a misogynistic culture, Clare had the audacity to speak of women as created fully in God's image and able to attain the same level of spiritual devotion as their male counterparts. Clare saw "herself as an image of God and capable of union with God because the Word became flesh and she herself was flesh."[24] Created in God's image, Clare saw herself as revealing God's glory and glorifying God by her very existence as a human being. Against the religious protocols of her time, Clare was the first woman to obtain papal approval of a rule she wrote for her order. In her intimacy with Christ, Clare grew in stature and found her authority as the leader of a religious movement. She became a spiritual pathfinder for both men and women, showing us how to give birth to Christ in the world by mediating his self-emptying love to the world around us.

Clare reminds us that the divine image present in all humanity requires us to go beyond social and political polarization to seek equality for all people: women and men, elders and children, people of all races, and heterosexuals and the LGBTQ+ community. Her vision of a self-governing women's monastery challenges us to work to equalize opportunities for all people in every sector of the social order. One in Christ, we are all beloved and valued. Children of God, reflecting God's image, we are one in the Spirit and must also be one in relationship and affirmation. The quest for stature requires us to embrace humankind in all its wondrous diversity as a reflection of God's loving artistry and wisdom. A twenty-first-century Franciscan spirituality affirms basic human rights for all people and the opportunity for all to grow toward the vision God has for them. Followers of Christ have a sacred obligation to pave the way to wholeness for all our human kin, regardless of gender, age, social standing, or nation of origin. No doubt a twenty-first-century Clare would be a contemplative activist, standing with the marginalized and oppressed and proclaiming the full humanity of all God's children.

## From Scarcity to Abundant Living

It has been said that most people are possessed by their possessions. Like Zacchaeus the tax collector, we are so absorbed in making money to achieve financial security that we are willing to connive and cheat to secure the monetary resources and power we think will bring us happiness (see Luke 19:1–10). Many of us are like the wealthy farmer who builds a great barn after an abundant harvest, believing it will secure spiritual contentment, only to die the night the project is completed (see Luke 12:16–21). In trying to provide a secure and comfortable life for our families, we find ourselves working long hours, seldom spending time with our loved ones, and turning our back on the family values we espouse. We often build walls, whether in our neighborhood or at our nation's borders, to ensure our security from the threats of strangers and those who differ from us. In contrast to consumerism and materialism, then and now, Luke's version of the Beatitudes affirms "Blessed are you who are poor, for yours is the kingdom of God" (Luke 6:20b).

Many Americans believe that they can never have enough money and that true security is found in financial well-being. Francis and Clare embarked on a very different path. They saw holy poverty as the source of abundant life. This is how Clare expresses that belief:

> O blessed poverty, who bestows eternal riches on those who love and embrace her!
> O holy poverty to those who possess and desire you!
> God promises the kingdom of heaven and offers, indeed, eternal glory and blessed life!

O God-centered poverty,

whom the Lord Jesus Christ,

who ruled and now rules heaven and earth,

Who spoke and things were made,

Condescended before all else![25]

For Francis and Clare, poverty and simplicity were a choice, reflecting their commitment to God and humankind. They eliminated everything that might stand between themselves and following the way of Jesus. No doubt they were aware of the poverty that destroys body, mind, and spirit; this is not the poverty they glorified. As mystics, they would have experienced deep empathy and solidarity with those who suffer from injustice and poverty.

For Francis and Clare, spiritual poverty involved the interplay of simplicity and fruitfulness to let in God's light and reflect that light to others. We need to prune everything that prevents us from experiencing God's presence in our lives. We need to quiet the voice of conflict, lure of consumerism, attraction of recognition and fame, and lust for power and possession to hear the voice of God. We need to be sure that our lives touch the earth lightly, that we care for the planet and work to ensure that everyone has sufficient food and housing. We need to eliminate the detritus that sullies the doors of perception, trapping us in shadows rather than freeing us for God's sunlight.

Beyond the subtraction is glorious addition. Embracing holy poverty, God-centered poverty, we receive everything we need for a joyous life: "O blessed poverty, who bestows eternal riches on those who love…eternal glory and blessed life." We are at home wherever we go. With nothing to claim or gain, we have nothing to defend and no one to fear.

While most of us are unlikely to sell all we have, we can use our assets wisely and compassionately. North Americans can mindfully let go of the privilege, prosperity, and prestige that separate us from others and contributes to the poverty of millions of Americans and people across the globe. We can prune our activities and desires, focusing on relational and spiritual well-being ahead of financial well-being. We can advocate for governmental policies that address the widening gap between the wealthy and poor in our nation and across the globe. While in my case, I need a safe and comfortable environment to provide hospitality for my grandchildren, who spend many afternoons and overnights at our home, I can cultivate simplicity of lifestyle in my upscale Washington, DC, suburb. I can choose to eat lower on the food chain, decrease fossil fuel consumption, and contribute generously to programs that address economic and social needs. Those of us in privileged positions are called to focus our attention on our spiritual lives and let our daily lives, including our consumption and finances, be guided by our spiritual values. Joined with the divine vine, we will experience overflowing abundance and connection with all reality.[26]

*From Fear to Love*

Although Francis became known as the friend of lepers, going out of his way to embrace them with God's healing love, this wasn't always the case. Despite his good-heartedness, as a youth Francis had an abhorrence for any type of physical disfigurement. Those with disabilities, wounds, and scars may have reminded him of the fragility of life and his own mortality. In his own words, "nothing disgusted me like seeing the victims of leprosy." One day, however, he found himself unexpectedly facing a man disfigured by leprosy. He wanted to turn back, but a divine inclination caused him to change his mind. He dismounted, embraced the man with leprosy, gave him some coins, and went his way, with a "great happiness [pervading] his whole being."[27] Not content with overcoming his fear and disgust, Francis entered a leper colony, "the last refuge of human misery...begged their pardon for having so often despised them...distributed money to them and left only after kissing them all on the mouth."[28]

It has been said that the opposite of love is fear, not hate. Fear alienates us from those people whom we feel put us or our way of life at risk. Spreading fear motivates those who foment hate and incivility, who believe others are out to replace them at work or in the voting booth, who worry that undocumented immigrants, members of the LGBTQ+ community, and people of color will destroy our way of life. The gospel takes another route: "There is no fear in love, but perfect love casts out fear" (1 John 4:18a). Francis's fear of people with leprosy was transformed by God's love. No longer bound by fear, Francis's heart opened, and every place became a gateway to divinity. His cramped soul became cosmic, filled with the love that created the galaxies, stars, and the good earth in all its wondrous variety. When we commit ourselves to embracing God's universal love, every place becomes home and every person God's beloved child. We transcend enmity and alienation and become Christ-bearers wherever we go.

### From Enemies to Friends

Francis lived in a time of great conflict among classes, cities, and villages, as well as between Christianity and Islam. Disputes were often settled by violence, whether in the Holy Land, the streets of Assisi, or between Assisi and its neighboring villages. When God touched Francis's heart, his parochialism was transformed to cosmopolitanism. He became a lover of all creation and the rainbow shades of human culture and religion. According to Bonaventure, "in all his discourses he proclaimed peace, saluting the people at the beginning of his sermons, with these words 'God give you his peace,' having learned this salutation (as he afterwards declared) by divine revelation." Francis commanded his followers to "proclaim peace to all men [sic]."[29]

Francis's commitment to peace led him to risk his life to reach out to a Muslim (Saracen) sultan, Malik al-Kamil, with whom he discussed the heart of Christianity and listened to the sultan's description of Islam. Francis mourned the death of Muslim fighters—despite their enemy status—and sought to be a healing presence in a time of war. The circle of love that embraced those with leprosy expanded to gather in those whom others would demonize as enemies. Inspired by Jesus's command to love one's enemies, Francis chose to see everyone, even the enemy, at the center of God's love and therefore worthy of his love.

### Spiritual Friendship

While Franciscan followers and biographers have described the friendship between Francis and Clare in a variety of ways, some accenting the spiritual and personal significance of their relationship, others downplaying it and minimizing Clare's role in Francis's life, the fact that their friendship is mentioned at all is frankly astounding. In the era of courtly love, regal women were put on a pedestal, objects of great romantic quests, and the inspiration of lovers' imaginations. Among those who exalted courtly love, only one type was conceivable: romantic and physical love. Seldom were women loved for their minds or spirits.

The love of Francis and Clare, and I believe they loved each other, was countercultural. It was a love grounded in spiritual stature, their own and the stature they saw in each other, reflected in wideness of vision and compassion. It was also a love that evolved. Clare, who described herself as Francis's "little plant," was, I suspect, at first intellectually and spiritually smitten by Francis, twelve years her senior. A richness of soul and passion of spirit shone through Francis. He articulated what was deepest in her spirit, but for which she had yet no words. Francis showed Clare the vision of holy poverty, a life directed solely to God. In spiritually grounded courtly fashion, Francis defended her, protecting her from her family who sought by force to return her to the world of courtly love and marriage. Yet, I believe that even at the beginning of their spiritual friendship, the relationship involved reciprocity. It is said that when the student is ready, the teacher comes. It is also true that when the right student comes along, the perceptive and spiritually attuned teacher finds fulfillment.

Over the years, the relationship between Francis and Clare evolved from teacher and student to peers and friends. Yet they were more than friends. When Francis was uncertain about whether to be a hermit or go on the road as an itinerant ambassador of Jesus, God directed him to consult Clare for spiritual guidance, and when Clare spoke, he listened and followed! She was no longer a little flower—she was a fully grown partner in ministry.

Legend has it that Clare and Francis once met for prayer, conversation, and a meal. The forest where they shared the afternoon lit up with such intensity that neighboring villagers believed that a fire had broken out, so great was the passion between Francis and Clare. Given Francis's and Clare's history, and Francis's devotion to the courtly love traditions, there may have been some physical temptation even between the saints of Assisi. They needed to ensure that the relationship was, above all, centered on God rather than their physical needs.

Later, Clare had a dream in which she was a small child, suckling at the breast of Francis. While I hesitate to interpret this dream from a contemporary psychological perspective, I believe that Clare's dream points to her deep intimacy with Francis. Spiritually speaking, they were "bone of my bone and flesh of my flesh." Francis's nurturing was vital to Clare's spiritual growth. Perhaps Francis felt the same about Clare. However we describe the relationship, in a time in which women were judged as spiritually inferior to their male counterparts, Francis and Clare were spiritual equals. Their relationship grew in wisdom and stature, and together they became more than they would have become alone, as they, like Jesus, found favor with God.

*From Personal Comfort to Redemptive Suffering and Solidarity*

The philosophical Bonaventure believed in the interdependence of theology and spirituality. Theology is grounded in mystical experiences, and mystical experiences are interpreted through theological reflection. The great religions of the world have their origins in mysticism, and the meaning of these primordial mystical experiences is articulated theologically.

As his life was waning, Francis prayed more fervently for a sense of God's presence in his life. In his contemplation, Francis was heartened to find that each time he opened the Scriptures, he came to the passion of Jesus. According to Bonaventure, "seeing that the book opened each time to the Passion of our Lord, the man of God understood that, as he imitated Christ in the actions of his life, so, that before he departed this world, he was to be conformed to Him likewise in the sufferings and pains of His Passion." On the Feast of the Exaltation of the Holy Cross, Francis received an angelic visitation, with a vision of Jesus stretched out on the cross. Francis realized that "he was to be transformed into Christ crucified, not by the martyrdom of the flesh, but by the fire of the Spirit." Nails appeared piercing Francis's hands and a wound surfaced in Francis's side.[30]

The appearance of the stigmata was the culmination of Francis's quest to embody Christ in mind, body, and spirit. The presence of the stigmata, while inviting Francis to experience Christ's suffering, was not primarily about mortification or bodily denial, but about compassion and identification with Christ's suffering on behalf of wounded humanity. The stigmata reflected God's healing solidarity with embodied humanity, and Francis's embodiment of Christ's spirit in his relationships. Jesus's death was an act of love, not a mortification of the flesh. Jesus's death revealed God's willingness to share human suffering to redeem us from the consequences of sin, alienation, injustice, and death, and to assure us that nothing can separate us from the love of God (see Romans 8:38–39).

Francis's stigmata were a call to prayer and an invitation for the mystic to be God's companion in seeking salvation for all humankind. In identifying with Jesus's cross, Francis became an instrument of peace and healing, his pain inviting others to find healing and wholeness.

Typically, suffering contracts our experience and concern. We focus on our pain and debilitation and turn away from the suffering of others. This is normal, and not a call for judgment or shame. Francis's stigmata, his suffering with Christ, was an experience of *theosis, or* divinization, of finding God in his suffering, transforming pain into prayer, and growing rather than withering in spirit. The stigmata widened his spiritual and ethical concern and empathy. From beginning to end, Francis sought to follow Jesus in "growing in wisdom and stature," even in times of suffering. Seeing his suffering as God's suffering, Francis, like Jesus, discovered that pain can be a window into infinity and mortality can be the path to salvation.

### From Life to Death

Death is the great mystery, provoking our fear and anxiety, as well as inspiring our courage and hope. Facing mortality, we are challenged to number our days that we might gain a heart of wisdom. For Francis, who sought to imitate Christ's way in his living, the answer to death was in praising God in his dying, and in giving thanks for the gift of life and God's fidelity in the future. Francis's "Canticle of the Creatures" was written as his body was wasting away. Francis realized that the antidote to fear is love, and that death is transformed through praising God for God's wondrous creation, even creation embodied in aging and mortality.

Eventually, all of our medical interventions will fail before the great equalizer. Francis responded to his impending death through song. He asked his companions to chant the "Canticle of the Creatures," and as they concluded, he penned his hymn to death, not as an enemy, but as a sister and a path to everlasting life in companionship with Jesus.

Praise be to you, my Lord, through our sister Bodily Death,
From whom no one can escape....

How lovely for those who are found in your most Holy Will,
For the second death can do them no harm.

Francis and his companions sang so joyfully that a fellow priest urged them to maintain sacred silence, fearing that the future saint's lusty singing would set a bad example for lay people. Francis's critic believed that we should be serious and mournful at the moment of death, confessing our sins, rather than praising God. Francis, of course, kept on singing.

Francis invites us to see death as a holy adventure with God as our companion. The One who inspires the rising of swallows, sun, and moon inspires death to sing alleluia at the doors of life everlasting. We can have faith for today, lived out in acts of reconciliation, healing, and transformation, because we have a bright hope for tomorrow, knowing that the blessings of this life will continue in God's Great Beyond.

## FRESH SPIRITUALITY

Spiritual stature involves widening our circles of spiritual and ethical concern. It involves holding in contrast the many aspects of your life as well as the religious, economic, political, and relational and lifestyle diversity in your community. Individuals of stature embrace otherness and are willing to grow through their encounters. Stature is not relativism, but empathetic relatedness. When we make judgments related to others' behaviors and beliefs, or institutional and political choices, we are guided by love as well as critique. We recognize our moral and spiritual limitations as well as the moral and spiritual limitations of those whom we challenge. We realize that challenging injustice is necessary to liberate both oppressor and oppressed.

## Growing in Wisdom and Stature

In this exercise, prayerfully look back at your life, considering your images of God, relationships, vocation, and personal goals. You may choose to do this over several days. Journaling your responses may help you ground your insights.

How did you imagine God's presence in your life and God's character as a child? How do you imagine God today? In what ways do you need to grow in relationship to God, in your image of God and sense of God's presence in your life?

Looking back to your childhood, consider how your understanding of the give and take of relationships has grown over the years. In what ways do you need to grow today and in the future, relationally?

Beginning with childhood, visualize your images of vocation, the sort of person you wanted to be at various stages of your life. Where have you sensed a presence of God's call? Toward what adventures is God calling you at this season of your life?

Conclude each exercise with gratitude for God's presence in

your life, for past and present opportunities for growth, and for widening circles of growth and compassion in the future.

*Life-Changing Friendships*

In another spiritual life review, I invite you to reflect with gratitude on your closest friendships. Beginning with childhood, recall your closest friends. Visualize your relationships, perhaps focusing on a special moment that reflects your intimacy. Which relationships were most pivotal in your life? What gifts did you receive from these friendships? What gifts did you share with your friends?

Looking at your relationships today, how do you feel about the quality of your relationships? Do they nurture your spirit? Do you nurture the spirits of your friends? Who might you be called to nurture at this time of your life?

Give thanks for your friendships, past and present. Ask that you grow in your friendships and that the spiritual depth of your friendships deepens for your well-being and the well-being of your friends.

*Solidarity with the Crucified Christ*

In the spirit of Francis, ask Jesus to open your senses to the pain and joy of the world. Ask that the "doors of perception" be purified so that you can experience infinity in the midst of time, seeing the world through the eyes of Christ. Open to the pain

Christ felt on the cross and the pain felt today by God's children, human and nonhuman.

Throughout the day, whether in encounters, news feeds, or live broadcasts, be attentive to the joys and sufferings of life. Be especially attentive to the suffering that you observe personally. Ask how you can be God's companion in responding to the suffering and injustice of the world.

*Hope in God's Everlasting Love*

Francis experienced the sacredness of death and saw death as part of God's praiseworthy world. When you consider your own mortality and the mortality of those around you, what is your response? Do you have trust or anxiety, excitement or fear, as you ponder your own death?

Each day, take time to meditate on these two passages, one from Francis, the other from St. Paul.

> Praise be to you, my Lord, through our sister Bodily Death,
> From whom no one can escape....
> How lovely for those who are found in your most Holy Will,
> For the second death can do them no harm. (Canticle of
> the Creatures)

> For I am convinced that neither death, nor life, nor angels,
> nor rulers, nor things present, nor things to come,
> nor powers,

nor height, nor depth, nor anything else in all creation
will be able to separate us from the love of God in Christ
Jesus our Lord. (Romans 8:38–39)

Give thanks for the life you have lived, for each new day and the
fresh opportunities it brings, and for God's promise of everlasting
life in companionship with Jesus, Francis, Clare, and the saints
and your ancestors.

**FRESH PRAYER**

God, whose energy brought forth the Universe
in all its wonder and glory,
whose wisdom guided the evolutionary process,
whose love embraced humankind and all creation
in its beauty and waywardness,
bless my journey.
Help me to walk the path of Jesus,
growing in wisdom and stature each day,
expanding my circle of compassion,
and trusting you in all the seasons of life.
Amen.

# CHAPTER FIVE

# Green and Growing Prayer

It is no longer I who live, but it is Christ who lives in me. And the life I now live in the flesh I live by faith in the Son of God, who loved me and gave himself for me.

—GALATIANS 2:20

He was always with Jesus,
Jesus in his heart,
Jesus in his mouth,
Jesus in his ears,
Jesus in his eyes,
Jesus in his hands,
Jesus in his whole body.[31]

—THOMAS OF CELANO

African American mystic and activist Howard Thurman counseled, "Don't ask yourself what the world needs. Ask yourself what makes you come alive, and go do that, because what the world needs is people who have come alive." Fully alive people reveal God's glory, and their fiery spirits inspire them to transform the world.

Francis and Clare were fully alive and deeply passionate in their love for Christ, commitment to simplicity, solidarity with the poor, love for one another, and joy in the human and nonhuman world. They were passionately on fire for "God and all things." Burning with passion for gospel spirituality, the simple way of Jesus, and their spiritual companionship, Francis and Clare lit up a forest with their zeal when they gathered for conversation and prayer.

Francis and Clare reflect an alternative, world-affirming spirituality. The spiritual path taken by most monastics in the twelfth and thirteenth centuries could be described as a journey of ascent from earthly to heavenly things. In contrast to this path of world-denial, Francis and Clare took another path toward God. Their mysticism reflected a "horizontal ecstasy," in which the journey inward and the journey outward are one and the same. Going deep within, they purified their passion, enabling it to be an aid instead of a hindrance to spiritual maturity.

## *A Spirituality of the Senses*

For Francis and Clare, the universe was a sacrament and revelation of the divine. The invisible and infinite God manifests through the visible world of sight as well as through the other senses. God addresses us in the songs of larks and swallows, the setting sun and rising moon, the verdant earth, and every human and nonhuman creature. While God can never fully be encompassed by our thoughts and theologies, God is not outside the world, acting only occasionally and supernaturally. God is within the world, incarnate, albeit often hidden, in every creature. God comes to us through every sense. We hear God's voice in chirping birds. We feel God's skin in the touch of a loved one. We taste and see God in freshly baked bread. We smell God in salty air at the beach, incense in worship, and the fragrance of rosemary and eucalyptus on our morning walks. God is the beyond that is also within us and among us in our bodies, minds, and spirits, and the bodies, minds, and spirits of our fellow creatures.

The journey inward and outward are one. Meditation leads to marvel. We might imagine Francis and Clare reveling in the photographs from the Hubble and Webb telescopes. They would delight in looking over Dr. Anthony Fauci's shoulder to the discover the power of vaccines to prevent coronavirus and human papilloma virus infection. Bonaventure noted that in beautiful things, Francis saw Beauty. Spiritual practices, even those that seem to draw us away from the world through asceticism and simplicity of life, can awaken us to the deep beauty of divinity.

## *Moment by Moment*

Francis's spiritual life evolved from a commitment to praying to becoming a prayer. Each moment God addresses us, inviting us toward full humanity and solidarity. While God's being cannot be encompassed by human experience, the immanence of God is not only in the world of sights and sounds, but also in our hearts and minds. God's still, small voice whispers in the storm of passion, the chaos of temptation, the anxiety of conflict, and the calm of contemplation.

We have seen that the key moments of Francis's life involved the interplay of divine call and human response. These are not rare encounters with God. Francis believed that God guides us each moment of the day, and that we can attune ourselves to God's way by making our whole lives a prayer. By placing ourselves in God's presence throughout the day, as Clare counseled Agnes of Prague, we experience God as the reality in whom we "live and move and have our being" (Acts 17:28). Francis opened to God in every encounter. Synchronicity abounds, and when we live prayerfully, every interchange and choice become an opportunity to experience God's wisdom guiding our daily lives. Spiritual practices open our whole being to God's call.

Today, with Clare, I can "place [my] mind in the mirror of eternity," doing God's will and trusting that God will treasure my efforts and that nothing "will be able to separate [me] from the love of God" (Romans 8:39). Embracing God in the holy here and now, each moment shares in God's everlasting life.

### Gazing and Praising

Certain sayings of Francis and Clare have become spiritual mantras for us, phrases we repeat over and over to center our spirits and deepen our faith. Once more, we hear Clare's words to Agnes of Prague. They are also her words to us, and God's counsel to anyone who wants to follow in the footsteps of Jesus.

Gaze upon Christ,

Consider Christ,

Contemplate Christ,

As you desire to imitate Christ.

We become like the objects of our attention. Where our hearts incline, our spirits will go. The focus of our attention, our ultimate concern, defines who we are and what we will become. Francis and Clare both sought to imitate Christ. They gazed upon the cross and conformed themselves to God's suffering love. In Christ, they saw divinity in the flesh and the glory of God in a fully alive human. They wanted to become fully alive, fully attuned, to the way of Jesus, whose Incarnation, ministry to outcasts, hospitality to strangers, practice of holy simplicity, and commitment to healing became the template for their own lives. Jesus's command to sell all and give to the poor guided their economic lives and relationships with the vulnerable.

Jesus's embrace of those considered unclean motivated their ministry to those with leprosy and society's outcasts. Christ is not confined to the first century; Christ is alive in our heart, mind, and hands. We meet Jesus in every encounter, from the person with leprosy on the roadside to the refugee parent seeking sanctuary in our nation. Our choice to follow his way—to gaze, consider, contemplate, and imitate—enables us to embody Christ in our lives. Jesus is not dead; he is resurrected and alive in all things, and he can burst forth when we claim, "It is no longer I who live, but it is Christ who lives in me" (Galatians 2:20).

### Spiritual Solidarity

Clare and Francis saw prayer as the source of spiritual stature. Prayer connects us with "God and all things." Everything is treasured in the heart of God. Prayer expands our empathy. The pain of others becomes our pain. The joy of others becomes our joy. Bearing the wounds of Christ, as Francis did, breaks open our defended hearts so that we embrace, and don't turn away from, the suffering of the world.

In Francis's and Clare's time, the experience of others' suffering was direct and personal. They encountered the despised and impoverished person with leprosy on the road. They heard the voices of children begging for alms as they walked the streets of Assisi. The bond of fear uniting the people of Gubbio with the vicious wolf called forth the desire for reconciliation. Today, we also experience the pain of others; for example, when we hear a grandchild crying or encounter a friend caring for a spouse with Alzheimer's disease or meet a young mother whose husband is dying of cancer. Our experience of pain is global as well as intimate, as we view events around the world in real time. This universal pain can be so great that we shut down emotionally because we see ourselves and our efforts as too small and inconsequential to make a difference. Franciscan spirituality reminds us that our prayers connect us to all creation and that even something as apparently insignificant as a prayer can open our hearts and hands and tip a situation from death to life. Going inward, we awaken to our pain and the pain of the universe and receive guidance to respond to the overwhelming crises of climate change, poverty, starvation, incivility, and racism. Prayer leads to solidarity and compassion and expands our circle of influence so that one child at a time, one call to a political representative at a time, one sacrificial gift at a time, one act of simplification at a time, the world is healed.

## Fresh Spirituality

The Muslim mystic Rumi delighted in proclaiming that there are a hundred ways to kneel and kiss the ground. God personally addresses us and inspires practices unique to our own lives as well as practices grounded in the traditions of Christianity and other faiths. Prayer opens us to a larger world, in which are constantly growing in wisdom and stature, and step by step drawing nearer to God's vision for us. God calls us moment by moment and encounter by encounter; our prayers and actions are our response. We are always on holy ground, whether distributing alms, writing a monastic rule, caring for grandchildren or aging parents, interacting on Zoom, or composing a poem or a memo. We can practice the presence of God in every life situation, joyful or repetitive, peaceful or contentious. Like Francis, we have the ability to make our whole lives a prayer.

*Every Breath a Prayer*

My prayer life has been enriched by practicing breath prayer. As a graduate student, I learned a simple prayer taught by Congregationalist minister Allan Armstrong Hunter:

> I breathe the Spirit deeply in,
> And blow it gratefully out again.

Now, over forty years later, I still employ this prayer in my daily walks and in times of conflict to keep me centered on God's Spirit and not my own anxiety, fear, defensiveness, or temptation. Years later, I learned a breath prayer from Vietnamese spiritual teacher Thich Nhat Hanh, known for joining action and contemplation in his engaged Buddhism:

Breathing in,
I feel calm,
Breathing out,
I smile.

I now use Thich Nhat Hanh's prayer, along with the Peace Prayer of St. Francis, to teach my middle-school grandchild how to be mindful of his behavior, find peace in the busyness of school and sports, and respond to preteen anxiety and conflict.

Francis provides a complementary breath prayer, which enables me to see God in myself and also in all creation. As I walk in my Potomac, Maryland, neighborhood at sunrise, I breathe deeply, and say the word, "God," as I inhale, and "and all things" as I exhale, opening my senses to the wonderful world around me, the moon setting, the brightness of sunrise, the glorious green of trees and lawns, the chirping birds. As I breathe Francis's words, I experience myself living in a God-filled world, in which divine inspiration can come to me around every bend and in every encounter.

As you go through your day's activities, try one of these breath prayers to make your whole day a prayer.

*Sensing Holiness*

From the beauties of the earth, we can experience God's deep beauty showing itself in all things. Whether you are homebound, hiking, or walking through your neighborhood, I invite you to let your senses roam with no clear goal other than noticing the world around you. Let your senses drift to whatever catches your attention.

This hot August morning, as I walked in the cool of the day, I gazed, in Clare's fashion, at the world around me with the eyes of Christ, feeling my connection with a mother deer and her two fawns, a bird chirping her morning song of praise, a neighbor walking her dachshund. I delighted in the morning sun and gave thanks. I felt the prayerfulness of movement, my feet rhythmically touching the pavement.

I came home to my study and alternated my attention from my computer to the grand oak trees, scudding clouds, and flying birds outside my window, and gave thanks.

Practicing God's presence is not difficult. It is simply a matter of attending to the graceful interdependence that gives life to all creation and enables you to experience this one unrepeatable moment.

*Walking with Jesus*

Movement is an important part of Franciscan spirituality. This practice can be done sitting in a chair or on the move. Take time for the following:

• Breathe deeply and slowly, perhaps using a breath prayer noted above.

- Ask Jesus to be your companion and reveal himself to you.
- Then, whether you are walking, sitting, or lying down, visualize Jesus beside you.
- Image yourself and Jesus joined in conversation and united in spirit.
- Share your spirit, emotions, thoughts—whatever is on your heart—with Jesus.
- Listen to his response, whether verbal or non-verbal.
- If you feel inclined, ask Jesus a question, and then listen for his response in this moment and throughout the day.
- Ask Jesus to walk beside you in the day ahead and for the sensitivity to know that he is with you.
- Conclude with a moment of prayerful gratitude.

*Gazing Prayer*

Clare's most well-known spiritual counsel was her guidance to Agnes of Prague:

> O most Noble Queen,
> Gaze upon Christ,
> Consider Christ,
> Contemplate Christ,
> As you desire to imitate Christ.[32]

Clare advised this spirituality of gazing, focusing on the life of Christ and, most significantly, the cross of Christ, as revealing

Jesus's intimate love for all creation and for each person. Gazing begins with the senses, transforms our heart and mind, and inspires our hands to reach out to those Christ loved.

In this exercise, choose a visual image of Jesus (painting, cross, icon) and gaze upon it, opening to its meaning in your life. Let the image invite you to contemplation of the reality behind the image, the Living Christ. Feel your unity with Christ, and experience his love pouring over you, filling you in mind, body, and spirit. Let Christ dwell in you as your deepest reality, joined in spiritual unity, filling your cells as well as your soul, bringing healing and wholeness to mind and body, and energizing your spirit.

Out of this deep gazing, ask Christ for guidance in ways to imitate him in your daily life, encounters, values, and citizenship. Listen for responses throughout the day.

*Spiritual Alchemy*

Prayer transforms us, raising our finite lives to infinity and our fallibility to gracefulness. Clare counsels Agnes of Prague:

> Place your mind before the mirror of eternity!
> Place your soul in the brilliance of glory!
> Place your heart in the figure of the divine substance!
> And transform your whole being into the image of the
> Godhead itself through contemplation.[33]

In stillness, experience yourself filled with divinity with every breath. Rest your whole being in the Ground of Being and Becoming, feeling God's energy flowing into your cells and soul. Open yourself to God's wisdom permeating your thoughts and attitudes, letting Christ be the source of your well-being, success, and personal agency. Feel the Christ in you emerging, illuminating, and guiding.

Throughout the day, train your eyes on eternity in the midst of time, divine brilliance in fallible humanity—your own and others'—and love that connects with all creation. Carry the phrase "God and all things" with you throughout the day to keep your vision of God's glory in every situation. Imagine yourself humbly becoming the image of God in all your relationships.

**FRESH PRAYER**

God of change and glory,

God of time and space,

give me the grace of passion.

Enflame me with love for this good earth

and all its creatures.

Purify my senses,

that my delight with embodiment and creation

may inspire generosity and compassion.

Let love and light burst forth,

warming and enlightening my spirit,

and giving light to all around me

and glory to God, my Creator and Loving Companion.

Amen.

# CHAPTER SIX

# *Fresh Church*

Awe came upon everyone, because many wonders and signs were being done through the apostles. All who believed were together and had all things in common; they would sell their possessions and goods and distribute the proceeds to all, as any had need. Day by day, as they spent much time together in the temple, they broke bread at home and ate their food with glad and generous hearts, praising God and having the goodwill of all the people. And day by day the Lord added to their number those who were being saved.

—ACTS 2:43–47

Then, all of a sudden, he heard a voice coming from the cross and telling him three times, "Francis, go and repair my house. You see, it is all falling down."[34]

—BONAVENTURE

Three years before his death, Francis held a celebration that changed the face of Christmas forever. A person of the people, whose ministry reached out to peasants as well as the privileged, Francis decided to celebrate Christmas with imagery and action in addition to the words and rituals of the Mass. Having obtained permission for his liturgical innovation from the pope, Francis and his companions "prepared a manger, and brought hay and an ox and an ass, to the place appointed." Francis summoned his followers and all the people of Greccio, and as "the people ran together, the forest resounded with their voices, and the venerable night was made glorious by many and brilliant lights and sonorous Psalms of praise. Francis chanted the Christmas story following Mass, and then told the story of the Babe of Bethlehem." People had visionary experiences, animals were cured of diseases, and people experienced miraculous healings, according to Bonaventure.[35] For the first time in their lives, many worshipers experienced the Incarnation as the living reality of God-made-flesh sharing the joys and sorrows of the human condition. The Nativity was no longer merely a story of a bygone era but the living revelation of God with us as one of us, a little child full of grace and peace and healing for humankind.

The simplicity of the manger and Francis's words proclaimed the beauty of Incarnation and affirmed God's presence in the experiences of common people as well as the priestly rituals of the church. The Word was made flesh in Greccio, and God's Word is made flesh in all creation, human and nonhuman alike. The Incarnation affirms a democracy of revelation and mission, grounded in the affirmation: "The true light, which enlightens everyone, was coming into the world" (John 1:9).

While Francis and Clare venerated the cross of Jesus and saw their own sacrificial lives as cruciform in nature, they saw the Incarnation of the Word and Wisdom of God as the primordial revelation of God. God's voice resounds in our praises, and we can see God's face everywhere and in everything. Just as Christ is larger and more expansive than Christianity, and is cosmic and universal in nature and influence, Francis and Clare as mystics and saints are larger than the Roman Catholic Church or any other Christian denomination. The saints of Assisi belong to and inspire everyone who seeks to live in the style of Jesus, following his way in the adventures of daily life and citizenship, regardless of ritual or creed. Even an iconoclastic, non-hierarchical Protestant like myself can experience wisdom and guidance from Francis and Clare.

Francis and Clare were reformers and the precursors of the movements that gave birth to the sixteenth-century reformation of Christianity. Faithful and obedient to the church of their birth and its leadership, their lives challenged an institution that had forgotten its gospel roots and traded simplicity for wealth and power. The quest for power and privilege was a temptation in the twelfth and thirteenth centuries and is still a temptation in our time. Religious institutions aligned themselves with powerful potentates in Germany during the 1930s, with Central American landowners and dictators in the late twentieth century, and with white nationalist provocateurs and political demagogues in the twenty-first-century United States of America. The church has often chosen the warlike Constantine over the healing Christ, and the coercive power of Caesar over the simple and welcoming Galilean. The church has often rejected the power of the gospel for what Franciscan scholar Leonardo Boff calls the gospel of power. While religious institutions always exist in economic and political contexts, the calling of Christian spiritual communities is, first and foremost, to follow the way of Jesus and the message of the prophets rather than the pomp and circumstance of political and corporate leaders.

### Francis and Clare as Quiet Challengers of the Church

Saints and mystics are often viewed as troublemakers by the religious and institutional powers of their times, even if their intention is to be loyal servants of these institutions, seeking to guide them to recover their spiritual bearings. Mysticism leads to mission, and mission always challenges the status quo with the vision of God's new creation. The lifestyle and values of saints and mystics transcend parochial understandings of Christian theology and ecclesiology and critique the imperfections inherent in the conservatism of religious structures and institutions. Although inspired by spiritual values, religious organizations have an interest in maintaining the economic, ecclesiastical, and administrative status quo and social order upon which their survival and flourishing depend.

Too much change is always a threat to institutional order. Consider Oscar Romero and Dorothy Day, and the institutional responses to their quests for social justice. Reflect on the responses from Catholic traditionalists to the liturgical and social innovations of Pope John XXIII and Vatican II. Conservatives object to the inclusive spirit of Pope Francis in his care for the environment as well as his outreach to women, the LGBTQ+ community, and indigenous peoples. Consider the responses of conservative Protestants and Muslims to changes in the social order and advances in science and medicine.

Clare and Francis were no exception to the prophetic spirit of mysticism. Though beatified and declared saints shortly after their deaths, during their lives they were a source of irritation and concern among powerful prelates, and their simplicity was an implicit critique of institutional religion. Living by gospel values calls into question every religious and political system, even those institutions that seek to be faithful to the teachings and life of

Jesus. The ideal of simplicity and poverty is always a challenge to an opulent, powerful, and tradition-oriented church.

The institutional church of Francis's and Clare's time promoted values vastly different than holy poverty and the peaceful relationships of the Assisi saints and the Jesus they sought to imitate. Pope Innocent III was the champion of the principle of "two swords," the doctrine that church was sovereign over both the religious and political realms of life. He envisioned a papal state in which the church was the primary secular authority. He ousted the Italian emperor and banished his officials from pontifical states. He dethroned the German monarch Philip of Swabia and put his throne in the hands of Philip's rival Otto of Bismarck, whom he later deposed in favor of Frederick II. Holding the keys of heaven, the papal threat of excommunication kept secular rulers in line and ensured a steady stream of income to Rome. Indeed, at the time that Francis, Clare, and Bonaventure lived, the Church of Rome held title to over half of the land holdings on the European continent. Although many priests lived in poverty, other prelates sold benefices, rewards in exchange for services to loyal nobles. These prelates lived in luxury, supported by their ability to reward loyal princes and business leaders with heaven and punish reformers and challengers with hell. Still, some nobles fought against papal authority and greed, risking excommunication and the threat of hell to ensure their independence from papal control. Growing antagonism to the church's power, wealth, and ecclesiastical domination in the twelfth and thirteenth centuries were crucial in setting the stage for the sixteenth-century Protestant Reformation.

Francis's vision of a church of the people, grounded in honoring poverty and simplicity, initially was met with a chilly reception by Innocent III. Clothed in the simplest tunic, Francis was mistaken for a swine herder by the regally attired Pope. When he heard Francis's request to form a religious order based on embracing Jesus's lifestyle of simplicity and sacrifice, the pope responded, "Leave me alone with your rule. Feed pigs instead. You can preach your sermons to them." In the act of a *jongleur*, or fool for Christ, Francis rushed to a pigsty, covered himself with dung, and returned to the pope, requesting "My Lord, now that I have done what you have commanded, please be good enough to grant my request." Most of the cardinals opposed Francis's request to form a religious order, fearing that it would stir up the peasants and threaten church authority and wealth. Representing a minority viewpoint, the Cardinal of St. Paul defended Francis's request, "If we reject the poor man's request on such a pretext, would this not be to declare that the Gospel cannot be practiced, and so blaspheme Christ, its Author?" Eventually, Francis's request to form an order based on poverty and solidarity with the poor was approved by Rome.[36]

In the decades to come, Francis and Clare presented an alternative vision of Christianity, grounded in the evangelical spirit of prayer, service, simplicity, and equality. They challenged binary religion in their affirmation of the universality of divine revelation and the giftedness of all creation. Following the way of Clare and Francis counters the cultural expectations and values of every century in its vision of an adventurous, forward-moving, non-hierarchical, and open-spirited church.

Neither Francis nor Clare articulated a formal ecclesiology or doctrine of the church. They were concerned with living the gospel rather than creating inflexible structures. Simplicity and hospitality guided the formation of their communities. They let their actions define a new vision of Christianity, joining ancient wisdom with contemporary spirituality, and honoring spiritual experience and Christian lifestyle over institutional order, ecclesiastical authority, and doctrinal uniformity. These same values inspire new visions of church in our time of chaos, upheaval, and change. While we cannot go back to the twelfth or thirteenth century, we can imagine fresh visions of Franciscan spirituality for our time of pluralism, pandemic, political incivility, technology, social media, and planetary destruction.

The way of Francis and Clare invites us to explore what religious community can look like when the future of institutional religion is at stake in the Northern Hemisphere, as a growing number of people describe themselves as "spiritual but not religious"; "nones," unaffiliated and untutored in any religious tradition; or "interspiritual," following what they perceive to be the best spiritual practices and teachings from a variety of religious traditions. In the wake of the pandemic, amidst the rise of religious pluralism and the growing influence of authoritarian movements in religion and politics, the message of Jesus must be experienced in fresh and novel ways if it is to be compelling to a new generation of seekers and critics. Confident in its message while being equally humble in spirit, a fresh church must share good news and listen to the voices of others—as Francis did when he visited the sultan in Damietta, Egypt.

## Gospel Simplicity

There is no going back to the premodern world of Francis and Clare in terms of technology, transportation, economics, and governance. We live in complex times, defined by the internet, social media, and the emerging metaverse. The intimate locality of spiritual experience is defined by worldwide encounters with people of other faiths, moment-by-moment information gathering from the internet and cable news, political posturing, and the economic impact of decisions made across the globe. In one day, the average person in the Northern Hemisphere ingests more information than Francis and Clare did in a whole lifetime.

The richness of our interdependent planet and its cultures is also the source of confusion, anxiety, and uncertainty, and threatens our ability to call any place home. Religious institutions are caught up in the interplay of dynamic interdependence and technological transformation, in which the media we use to share our faith shape our message, and at times the medium becomes the message itself, distorting the simple, spiritually grounded, and hospitable message of Jesus of Nazareth. Just as the early Franciscans sought to share the first-century evangelical spirit of simplicity in their own thirteenth-century ways, our going forward must find direction in embracing ancient wisdom in partnership with God's forward-looking invitation to become new creations.

For Francis and his companions, the key innovative element in spiritual transformation was gospel simplicity, the deep desire to live the way of Jesus in their time. The Franciscan quest for simplicity was countercultural in spirit and revealed an alternative vision of spirituality for householders and business people as well as men and women living in religious community. They understood that the many tasks required of them and their openness to reformation in terms of gospel simplicity was grounded in one thing alone: their imitation of the simple Galilean. Their fresh vision focused on the unity of creation, solidarity with suffering, flexible and practical spiritual practices, and the willingness to see all people—and all creation—as kin. Gospel simplicity invited them to exert the all-embracing power of the Spirit rather than the stifling spirit of power.

In our time, we have discovered that the personal is the political and the political is the personal, and this means that faith communities must be involved in the healing of the larger society as well as maintaining their own spiritual integrity and vitality. The interdependence of creation and the direct and pervasive life-and-death impact of governments and corporations on millions of people make involvement in society a necessity for both individuals and religious institutions. Living simply and spiritually in a complex and contentious environment is the challenge to being a fresh church today. The world wants to see a church that provides an alternative to our society's values, while caring for the planet and its institutions. The world needs to see churches that join prophetic challenge with care for those whose policies they are challenging.

Churches as institutions, whether in terms of congregations or denominations, have boundaries, histories, and traditions to maintain. Today's churches are also part of the societies in which they dwell, and recipients of the goodwill of societies as charitable organizations and promoters of morality appropriate to good citizenship. But the boundaries and social context of churches should not be an impediment to self-criticism and transformation of church and society. A fresh church, grounded in the spirit of gospel simplicity, must be in and not of its society and its values. It must present a higher aspiration and alternative value system than the values of consumerism, profit-making, power politics, and the inevitable coercion necessary for the maintenance of social order.

A church grounded in the Franciscan spirit of simplicity must first challenge its own tendency toward self-interest and survival as primary values. It must humbly recognize its limitations and temptations to focus on survival and maintaining tradition for its own sake, while being open to discover truths outside its theological, liturgical, and spiritual walls. It must be a church for others, whose institutional decision-making and congregational preaching encourage simplicity, sharing, and downward economic mobility among those who are economically privileged. Its power must be the power of the ideal, revealed in loving relationships, not the power of doctrinal and ecclesiastical coercion, enforced by clerical hierarchies. It must be willing to put its own institutional survival at stake for the sake of the world God loves.

Gospel simplicity ironically affirms the reality of diversity and pluralism in the surrounding culture as well as the pluralism within the church itself. The humility of gospel simplicity recognizes that there are many forms of Christianity, grounded in a variety of religious experiences, cultures, ethnicities, and traditions. A simple gospel embraces the complexity of perspectives, focusing on orthopraxy, ethical action, and spirituality, rather than on enforced orthodoxy or doctrinal correctness. There is room for householders and monastics, priests and laypeople, civil servants and prophets, traditionalists and innovators, working together for God's glory and the well-being of humankind and creation. The commitment to "God and all things" comes first, while our own egos, self-interest, and institutional structures are secondary. The diversity of flora, fauna, earth, sea, and air, so beloved by Francis, awakens us to the wondrous diversity of humankind and the nonhuman world and the need to protect the diverse expressions of human spiritual experience. Diversity is not a fall from grace, but the expression of God's abundant life, wisdom, and creativity.

Gospel simplicity sees the church's mission as joining inward spirituality with outward service. Sacrifice, not security, is its polestar, and the "least of these" beloved by God are the object of its concern. Loving all God's people, the church, inspired by Franciscan spirituality, means having a preferential option for the poor, while recognizing that justice-seeking is essential for the spiritual health of the wealthy and powerful, whose souls are jeopardized by their injustice and consumerism.

## Spiritual Democracy

Francis and Clare proclaimed a deep spiritual democracy, which fully embraced the human and nonhuman world as partners in God's mission, as evidenced in the Canticle of the Creatures. Whatever can be praised as God's handiwork, whether geological, meteorological, anthropological, or biological, deserves our spiritual and ethical consideration. Moreover, whatever can praise God in the creaturely world in response to life's blessings is a vehicle of divine revelation, open to and able to channel divine inspiration.

Fresh church promotes cosmopolitan spirituality. All God's creatures give praise to their Creator. In the Hebrew Scriptures, the patriarch Jacob awakens from a dream of angels ascending and descending a ladder from earth to heaven and back again and stammers, "Surely the Lord was in this place—and I did not know it." He names the place "Beth-El," the house of God (see Genesis 28:10–22). God's sanctuary and sacramental presence is within the walls of church buildings and throughout the whole earth. The world beyond cathedral and sacrament is the primary sacrament of God. Our liturgical sacraments serve to awaken us to the sacramental, or holy, nature of life itself. Priests, pastors, imams, rabbis, shaman, and rishis have unique roles in religious communities as spirit people whose task is to awaken the Spirit in their communities. Spiritually awakened laypeople can convey divine blessings and wisdom that often eludes the clergy and spiritual functionaries of their faith traditions. Within Franciscan communities, different gifts lead to different responsibilities, but priests and laypeople are equals in mission and service.

Fresh church delights in the universal vocational spirit envisioned by St. Paul in his first letter to the Corinthians:

> Now there are varieties of gifts, but the same Spirit; and there are varieties of services, but the same Lord; and there are varieties of activities, but it is the same God who activates all of them in everyone. To each is given the manifestation of the Spirit for the common good. To one is given through the Spirit the utterance of wisdom, and to another the utterance of knowledge according to the same Spirit, to another faith by the same Spirit, to another gifts of healing by the one Spirit, to another the working of miracles, to another prophecy, to another the discernment of spirits, to another various kinds of tongues, to another the interpretation of tongues. All these are activated by one and the same Spirit, who allots to each one individually just as the Spirit chooses (1 Corinthians 12:4–11).

Everyone has gifts, and all gifts are important for the community's well-being. We need one another. The graceful interdependence of life requires many gifts and vocations. The church is a laboratory for vocational service for itself and the world. To be complete and healthy, its members' gifts must be nurtured and fulfilled and shared with the wider world. Today, we would extend these gifts beyond the church and the human community. Swallows can be preachers and wolves can become guardians!

The cosmopolitan spirit of fresh church welcomes the wisdom of the world's great religious traditions as complementary to Jesus's message of healing and wholeness. Every religious tradition is a divine center reflective of divine wisdom and insight and can be a vehicle of salvation for its participants. Francis visited a Muslim sultan to share the gospel, and the two of them engaged in a lively give-and-take that enlarged both of their spirits. Today, we need to engage other spiritual traditions with humility, willing to share our insights and learn from our conversations. Common ground with other faiths is necessary if our planet is to find healing. Learning from other faiths is as imperative as learning from other cultures in the ongoing vitality of fresh church.

### Faithful Equality

As I have asserted throughout this book, the relationship of Francis and Clare affirms the faithful equality of women and men in the church and the world. While Francis was initially Clare's teacher and mentor, she became his spiritual companion and the leader of a religious order in her own right. Francis sought Clare's spiritual counsel in helping him discern the shape of his ministry. Clare assertively petitioned to develop a rule of absolute poverty for her order and received papal approval of that rule shortly before her death. Knowing that she was created in the image of God, Clare recognized her full humanity and the full humanity of all women and claimed her gifts as a spiritual leader and model.

Fresh church in the Franciscan spirit challenges any binary understanding of humankind. In Christ, the distinctions that divide people are irrelevant to human wholeness and adventurous communities. Binary religion with its insiders and outsiders looks backward to the "good old days" of institutional power and privilege, while spiritual adventure looks forward toward God's peaceful realm. Adventurous spirituality affirms that all are beloved and gifted to love and serve, and to be cherished and served. If God's center is everywhere, as Bonaventure asserts, then every person is equally centered by God, regardless of gender, sexual identity, race and ethnicity, intelligence, age, or nation of origin. Our calling is to help our kin find their unique spiritual center as their unrepeatable gift to the world. God speaks in the voices of infants and elders, Europeans and Afghans, gay theologians and heterosexual organists, New Englanders and Somalians, celibate priests and married parents.

### Solidarity with Suffering

For Francis and Clare, there is no "other." We are all one in the Spirit. There is a continuity of joy and suffering that embraces all creation, human and nonhuman. What happens to refugee children, Ukrainian parents, right whale pups, and polar bears on ice caps matters to us because in the intricate interdependence of life, our joys and sorrows are one.

Rich and poor, human and nonhuman, are joined in God's wondrous creation. Whether in a monastery or on the road, our joys and sorrows are one. Fresh religious communities have open doors, hearts, and hands. They reach out, as Francis did, to all people, overcoming revulsion, judgment, and alienation to see Christ in them and be Christ with them. In an interdependent world, the most pitiable—and dangerous—person and institution is the one that believes its well-being is isolated from the well-being of the community and the planet. Notions of "me first," "congregation first," and "nation first" ultimately go against our personal, congregational, national, and planetary well-being; they also go against the structure of God's world, where individuality and community, solitude and relationship, cannot be separated. From this perspective, the inner and outer are one in the spiritual journey and the mystic's experience. The church that prays is also the church that sacrifices and risks its own reputation to stand with the poor.

Legend has it that on one of his journeys, Francis encountered a pilgrim. He asked his new companion, "Brother, speak to me of God." Without saying a word, the pilgrim guided Francis to a city, where the pilgrim sat down, opened his knapsack, and distributed bread to the women and children, who ate until they were full. As they passed the bread around, the loaves were miraculously multiplied so that everyone, kin and stranger, young and old, male and female, had enough to enjoy and share. As the feast concluded, the pilgrim gazed at the sky and said, "Our Father," and then paused a moment to proclaim, "Our bread." Francis was overjoyed, for he met God in the sharing of bread among the poor, who in turn shared it among themselves.[37]

Liberation theologian Leonardo Boff describes Francis's and Clare's vision of holy poverty as the "evangelical way of life," a life of "total availability" to the poor and marginalized.[38] Spirituality and service are one. When we pray, we transform the world. When we serve, we transform our prayers. When we walk for justice, "our legs are praying," as Rabbi Abraham Joshua Heschel described his civil rights marches with Martin Luther King Jr. It has been noted that outsiders, often described as "spiritual but not religious" or "nones," love Jesus but are alienated from the church. Fresh church in the Franciscan spirit lets go of what liberation theologians describe as the "domination system": the systemic injustice, planetary destruction, and racism often perpetrated by institutions, motivated by binary, us-them and saved-unsaved understandings of reality. An adventurous church has a divine spiritual center energized by love, but no outside boundaries that exclude individuals by doctrine, liturgy, or rule. Fresh church abandons ecclesiastical, doctrinal, liturgical, economic, and racial domination to embrace a sacramental universe in which Christ dwells in each creature. In caring for those in need, even the spiritually bankrupt potentates and powermongers, we care for Christ and join Christ in healing the world.

## FRESH SPIRITUALITY

Francis was a person of study and prayer and encouraged reflection and contemplation among his followers. He also believed that the fruit of study and prayer is in service, almsgiving, and care for the vulnerable, poor, and forgotten. While fresh spiritual communities are careful financially, their primary goal is their mission to the world, to be a church of the poor and marginalized. Welcoming to all, fresh communities are called to be laboratories and sanctuaries of prayer and vocation, inspiring gifts for service to the world.

### God in the Least of These

Jesus joined mysticism and morals when he proclaimed, "Truly I tell you, just as you did it to one of the least of these who are members of my family, you did it to me" (Matthew 25:40). When we reach out to the poor and powerless, we are, in the words of Saint Teresa of Calcutta, doing "something beautiful for God." We embrace our solidarity with them, discover their unique giftedness, and enrich the life of God.

Dorothy Day discovered the solidarity of all life during her first arrest for protesting injustice. No longer set apart, "I was that mother whose child had been raped and slain. I was the mother who had borne the monster who had done it. I was even that monster who had done it."[39] She also realized that within God's earthly body, we are all one, "I was no longer a young girl, part of a radical movement seeking justice for those oppressed; I was the oppressed. I was that drug addict, screaming and tossing in her cell, beating her head against the wall."[40] Day's spirit was opened to "God and all things," as she found that "The mystery of the poor is this: That they are Jesus, and that what you do for them, you do for Him."[41] In this exercise, begin with a time of stillness. When you discern that your spirit is calm and open, reflect on the world in which you live. When and where have you seen the poor and marginalized? The forgotten and oppressed? As your doors of perception open, visualize each one as Jesus, wounded and abandoned, and see yourself providing Jesus, the poor one, with comfort, whether this comfort comes in the form of food and water, housing and clothing, or political advocacy. Experience Jesus's delight and gratitude at your generosity.

If you are a member of a religious community, consider when, if it all, your community interacts with the poor Jesus. Do you feed him or pass him by, focusing only on your rituals and survival? What do your congregation's values say about its commitment to bringing joy to Jesus and all God's children? Prayerfully reflect on one action your religious community can take to respond to the poor and forgotten. Give thanks for the opportunity to serve Christ in those around you.

### Embracing the Outcast

Francis's heart was transformed when he embraced a person with leprosy. He discovered God's presence in those whom he had once seen as disfigured and disgusting. He washed their wounds, kissed their lips, and spoke to them with reverence. Seven centuries later, Dorothy Day saw the spiritual side of activism in addressing everyone with respect, as she sought to "talk to men [*sic*] as if they were angels."[42]

Looking at your life, how does your speech reflect your spiritual values? Do you speak with respect, kindness, and compassion, especially in relation to the "others," those whom you perceive as different morally or spiritually than yourself—a person without a home, an undocumented worker, or a dishonest, power-hungry politician? How does your congregation speak of the "others" in your community? Make a commitment in your personal and community life to speak with honesty and respect, and let your words take shape in acts of kindness and generosity.

### Nurturing Equality in Community Life

All religious communities are historically and institutionally ambiguous. They begin with high aspirations reflected in acts of generosity and inclusion, grounded in the direct experience of God in their lives and the world. Over time, they may also create hierarchies and align themselves with economic and political powers that often dehumanize our kin in Christ. Francis and Clare set aside domination as they challenged hierarchies based on ordination, gender, economics, and power. "God and all things" meant that all things were treasured by God and deserved to be treated with ethical consideration and compassion.

Looking at your religious community, do you see hierarchical behaviors or decisions that dehumanize members of the community, treating them as "less than" the congregation's or denomination's implicit or explicit leadership? Do you participate in this hierarchical and binary behavior? Prayerfully confess your complicity in sexism, racism, ableism, economic injustice, or exclusion. Ask God to open your spirit to ways that you might encourage your congregation to be a house for all people, especially those who are considered religious or moral outsiders. Ask God for guidance in transforming your behavior and, in the spirit of Francis, repairing your broken religious community. Thank God for the opportunity to make a fresh beginning in creating a faithful and loving community.

### Fresh Prayer

Open my senses to the world's suffering.

Open my heart to God's pain in the pain of the world.

Open my hands to give selfless and generous service.

Open my tongue that I might speak to everyone

as if they were an angel,

addressing them with respect and compassion.

Let me see you, O Jesus, in all creatures,

and act always to bring beauty to your life and the world.

Amen.

CHAPTER SEVEN

# Refreshing Creation

Praise the Lord from the earth,

you sea monsters and all deeps,

fire and hail, snow and frost,

stormy wind fulfilling his command!

Mountains and all hills,

fruit trees and all cedars!

Wild animals and all cattle,

creeping things and flying birds!

Let everything that breathes praise the Lord!

Praise the Lord!

—PSALM 148:7–10; PSALM 150:6

Be praised, my Lord, through all your creatures,

especially through my lord Brother Sun,

who brings the day; and you give light through him.

And he is beautiful and radiant in all his splendor!

Of you, Most High, he bears the likeness.

Praise be You, my Lord, through Sister Moon

and the stars, in heaven you formed them

clear and precious and beautiful.

Praised be You, my Lord, through Brother Wind,

and through the air, cloudy and serene,

and every kind of weather through which

You give sustenance to Your creatures.

Praised be You, my Lord, through Sister Water,

which is very useful and humble and precious and chaste.

Praised be You, my Lord, through Brother Fire,

through whom you light the night and he is beautiful

and playful and robust and strong.

Praised be You, my Lord, through Sister Mother Earth,

who sustains us and governs us and who produces

varied fruits with colored flowers and herbs....[43]

—FRANCIS OF ASSISI

Jewish mystics note that if you save a soul, it is as if you have saved the world; if you destroy a soul, it is as if you have destroyed the world. Even the smallest of actions—hugging a person with leprosy, welcoming an undocumented worker as kin, choosing to eat lower on the food chain—can be a factor in transforming the world. The challenges we face today often seem beyond our capabilities, and we are tempted to give up hope, until we realize with Francis that the world is saved one act at a time, and we can turn the tides of life, individually and corporately, from hate to love and death to life.

At fifteen, Swedish high school student Greta Thunberg fell into depression after realizing that human actions were putting the planet at risk and that the world's political leaders were doing little or nothing to prevent ecological catastrophes that would threaten the well-being of her own and future generations. During August 2018, she began to sit in front the Swedish Parliament on Fridays, with a sign reading "School strike for climate." Her protest caught on, creating what was described as the "Greta Effect": one person, a diminutive teenager, inspiring thousands of other youth and adults to work for a better future. Small can be beautiful, and a little child can lead us!

Like Francis and Clare, Thunberg knows that our choices can be a matter of life and death for ourselves and the planet. We can act to save the lives of worms, sparrows, wolves, and future human generations by embracing simplicity at every level of life. We need to move from ignorance and apathy to agency and action. Thunberg challenges the leaders of the world and people like us.

The problem we are facing is not that we lack the ability to dream or imagine a better world. The problem now is that we need to wake up. It's time to face the reality, the facts, the science.[44]

Francis and Clare knew that the realm of God emerges from mustard seeds and marginalized people, that God uses the foolish of the world to shame the wise and powerful and call them to sacrifice for the vulnerable and forgotten. They knew that by their actions, as well as their counsel, they needed to be the voice of the voiceless, calling the church to follow Christ and heal the world. To those who scoff at the dream of a better world and the high calling of holy simplicity to save our planet, Francis and Clare join young Greta Thunberg's pleas addressing the powerful adults upon whom the future of our planet depends:

> You must do the impossible.
> Because giving up can never be an option.[45]

### Francis Speaks with Pope Francis

In June 2015, three years before Greta Thunberg began her protest, Pope Francis published the papal encyclical *Laudato Si': Care for Our Common Home*, patterned after St. Francis's "Canticle of the Creatures," challenging people of faith as well as seekers and agnostics to take swift action to respond to climate change. When he was elected pope in 2013, Cardinal Jorge Mario Bergoglio of Buenos Aires, Argentina, chose the name Francis to honor the life and work of Francis of Assisi, "the man of poverty, the man of peace, the man who loves and protects creation"[46] and "addressed creatures as 'sisters,' and 'brothers', that is, as equals, not subjects to be dominated."[47] People of power can choose humility and solidarity with marginalized people and the forgotten planet.

Pope Francis's *Laudato Si'* may be described as a theological, economic, and ethical reflection on Francis of Assisi's creation-oriented spirituality. *Laudato Si'* is also an institutional response, commissioned and written by the spiritual leader of Christianity's largest religious community. Pope Francis's encyclical is breathtaking in its theological and scientific insight, its recognition of ecological spirituality as essential to the Christian tradition, and its affirmation of the lifestyle of Francis of Assisi.

*"Laudato si', mi' Signore*—'Praise be to you, my Lord.' In the words of this beautiful canticle, St. Francis of Assisi reminds us that our common home is like a sister with whom we share our life and a beautiful mother who opens her arms to embrace us."

Pope Francis applauds Francis of Assisi as the "example par excellence of care for the vulnerable and of an integral ecology lived out joyfully and authentically. He is the patron saint of all who study and work in the area of ecology, and he is also much loved by non-Christians. He was particularly concerned for God's creation and for the poor and outcast." The life of Francis "shows us just how inseparable the bond is between concern for nature, justice for the poor, commitment to society, and interior peace."[48]

Francis of Assisi sought to be the daily embodiment of the vision he expressed in the "Canticle of the Creatures." To follow Jesus means to love God's creation, great and small. The Canticle's vision of a living, praising, loving universe inspires reverence for life and honoring of all creatures, great and small. The world is God's handiwork. God inspires and breathes through all things, even in their brokenness. Glory demands gratitude and a new kind of discipleship, grounded in our kinship with all creation.

Today's philosophers describe Francis's world of praise as the recognition that, while varied in complexity and sensitivity, experience is universal. All life forms interact with their environment, shaping and being shaped by their encounters. As a hymn of my childhood affirms, "all nature sings and around me rings the music of the spheres." Creation is alive from the cells of our bodies to the human spirit. Birds sing for joy. My goldendoodle, Tucker, delights in racing across open spaces. Humpbacked whales rejoice in their songs. Fireflies light up the sky in search of love. T-cells identify and neutralize viruses. Human experience is not solitary in the universe but a reflection of the varieties and levels of experience characteristic of life on our planet. Even flowers and trees have been found to interact with one another and the creatures around them!

Francis's incarnational spirituality inspired reverence in his interactions with the nonhuman world around him. Rather than penning a theology of ecology, Francis of Assisi embodied the vision of a living, experiencing, and interdependent universe in his interactions with the nonhuman world, from delighting in sparks of fire to teaching a predatory wolf to become the community's protector. He called the birds and animals brothers and sisters in Christ, as surely his kin as his human companions.

Thomas of Celano, Francis's first biographer, describes Francis's interactions with the nonhuman world as reflecting the greeting he gave to nonhumans and humans alike, "Peace be with you."[49] To the birds of the air, the ecological saint proclaimed, "My brother birds, you should greatly praise your Creator, and love him always," to which the birds "stretched their necks, spread their wings, open their beaks, and looked at him." Francis made a commitment to exhort "all birds, all animals, all reptiles, and also all insensible creatures, to praise and love their Creator." So delighted were swallows with a message that they began "shrieking and chirping," such that Francis had to admonish them, "My sister swallows, now it is time for me to speak, since you have already said enough. Listen to the word of God and stay quiet and claim until the word of the Lord is completed." Immediately those little birds fell silent. Francis liberated a rabbit caught in a trap, and then asked, "Brother Rabbit, why did you get yourself caught?" When "brother fish" was thrown back into the water, he stayed by Francis's boat, honoring the saint's kindness. Remembering the text, "I am a worm and not a man, [Francis] used to pick them up from the road and put them in a safe place so that they would not be crushed by the footsteps of a passerby." Even insects were the apple of Francis's eye: "In the winter, he had honey or the best wine put out for the bees so that they might not perish from the cold." Francis felt the joys and suffering of the nonhuman world, and, in turn, the nonhuman world responded with joy and obedience to Francis.

While we may judge stories of Francis's encounters with the nonhuman world as fanciful legends irrelevant to our technological society of factory farming and fisheries, I believe they are remembered history, reflecting the deep truth of pan-experientialism, the affirmation of the universality of experience and value. Thomas of Celano summarizes Francis's creation-affirming spirituality poetically:

> Fields and vineyards,
> Rocks and woods,
> and all the beauties of the field,
> flowing streams and blooming gardens,
> earth and fire, air and wind:
> all these he urged to love of God and to willing service.
> Finally, he used to call all creatures
> by the name of "brother" and "sister"
> and in a wonderful way, unknown to others,

he could discern the secrets of the heart of creatures

like someone who has already passed

into the freedom and glory of the children of God.[50]

As living and experiencing manifestations of God's wise creativity, nonhuman creatures are valuable apart from human uses and deserve our ethical consideration as well as spiritual care.

A few centuries after Francis's death, the Franciscan vision was relegated to the realm of religious superstition and irrelevance. Francis's theophanic vision of nature was replaced by the modern world's affirmation of Newton's lifeless, mechanical universe, Descartes's separation of mind and body and denial of creaturely experience, and deism's relegation of God to the role of an outside creator uninvolved in history, rather than the inner spirit guiding and nurturing the historical process. From this perspective, the insentient and mechanical nonhuman world was nothing more than a human resource, valuable only insofar as it supports human commerce and well-being. Consumption and manipulation of nature became the norm. Christianity's relationship with indigenous peoples and nonhuman creatures would have been quite different if Francis's vision had been affirmed as the underpinning of the scientific and technological adventures of European civilization. Instead of being seen as the culprit in ecological destruction, based on its dualism of humankind and nature, Christianity would have been the inspiration for earth-affirming and creature-honoring technology and science and appreciation of the wisdom of non-Western indigenous peoples.

Pope Francis's encyclical brings the spirit of Francis of Assisi into twenty-first-century ecology and economics.

> A living, breathing universe, praising God at every level of being, inspires awe and respect. The sacramental nature of life transforms our human vocation from one of domination to one of nurture and restoration. Tragically, we have threatened the foundations of life, and desecrated our mother and sister for economic gain and the prerequisites of power. This sister now cries out to us because of the harm we have inflicted on her by our irresponsible use and abuse of the goods with which God has endowed her. We have come to see ourselves as her lords and masters, entitled to plunder her at will. The violence present in our hearts, wounded by sin, is also reflected in the symptoms of sickness evident in the soil, in the water, in the air and in all forms of life. This is why the earth herself, burdened and laid waste, is among the most abandoned and maltreated of our poor; she "groans in travail" (Romans 8:22).[51]

A fresh vision of the nonhuman world, a re-enchantment of nature, inspires us to fresh human values. We are part of nature. We are companions and kin with all creation, affirming God's wise creativity beyond humankind. Every creature is thus the object of the Father's tenderness, who gives it its place in the world. Even the fleeting life of the least of beings is the object of his love, and in its few seconds of existence, God enfolds it with his affection…. The entire material universe speaks of God's love, his boundless affection for us. Soil, water, mountains: everything is, as it were, a caress of God.[52]

A fifteen-year-old non-religious high school student and a seventy-eight-year-old Catholic spiritual leader both reflect the world-affirming spirit of Francis of Assisi as an antidote to the destructive impact of unrestrained consumerism, economic injustice, and addiction to fossil fuels on our planet's well-being and humankind's future. Our survival depends on transformed thinking and feeling that gives birth to transformational action to heal the earth and its creatures. We need to change our worldview to embody a new set of values, grounded in gratitude and amazement at the intricate beauty and fragility of creation. Not bound to the thirteenth century, Francis provides a vision of a new earth, grounded in the kinship of all creatures as God's beloved children, that serves as inspiration to heal our planet from the devastation of human-caused climate change.

Embodying the vision of Franciscan simplicity is our calling, personally and institutionally. Economics and ecology are intimately connected. Injustice toward our fellow humans leads to destruction of the planet. Environmental destruction and climate change affects the poor and powerless, while currently causing only slight inconveniences to the privileged and powerful. Fidelity to God requires us to change our lifestyles, live more simply, transform the goals of our institutions from consumption to preservation, and claim humbly our roles as God's companions in healing the earth. While the success of our quest for environmental healing is not assured, our calling is to take up the task for God, our children and grandchildren, future generations we will never meet, and for our planet in all its wondrous diversity.

### God's Partners in Healing the World

Francis saw himself as a new kind of fool, God's fool, who sold all he had, gave his wealth to the poor, and in return discovered spiritual freedom and security. Clare discovered that downward mobility was the pathway to heavenly spirituality. In words that challenge the gods of consumerism and materialism, for whom growth and possession are the pathway to happiness, Clare praised holy poverty:

> O Holy Poverty,
> who bestows eternal riches on those who love and
> embrace her.
> O Holy Poverty,
> to those who possess and desire you
> God promises the kingdom of heaven
> and offers, indeed, eternal glory and blessed life.

O God-centered poverty.

whom the Lord Jesus Christ

Who ruled and now rules heaven and earth,

Who spoke and things were made,

Who condescended to embrace before all else.[53]

Following the way of Jesus, Clare and Francis trusted that those who put Christ's way first in their lives will receive a "hundred-fold in place of the one, and a blessed and eternal life."[54]

Francis and Clare ask us, "Will you embrace God's way, which brings peace and the experience of everlasting life to our daily lives, or a life of consumption and possession, which brings pleasure but also insecurity and anxiety about that which will eventually pass away?"

Francis and Clare challenge us to seek God's pathway of healing and peace, which is found in self-transcendence and kinship with all creation. Peace and healing come when we sacrifice self-interest, and the defensiveness that comes with it, for world loyalty, and the expansiveness that emerges when we love our neighbors as ourselves, not just spiritually but in our daily economic choices and commitment to healing the planet and its creatures.

The path is clear for us. There is no room for denial: our priorities have jeopardized the future of the planet, its diverse species, and future generations of human and nonhuman life. If we do not choose the path of simplicity, personally and politically, extreme weather will become the norm; oceans will rise, destroying coastal cities; millions will become refugees or die of starvation; water wars will emerge; the coral reefs and sea life will perish; polar ice caps will continue to melt; and eventually, ecosystems upon which life depends will collapse. This stark reality is recognized not only by tree-hugging environmentalists but also by multinational corporations, banking institutions, and the United States military, which is currently considering the likelihood of both climate wars and the threat of rising oceans to naval bases if we do not successfully respond to the dangers of climate change.

Now is the time to act, to choose a new pathway, to become fools for Christ and the planet. While we can't do everything, we can do something: we can live more simply, using fewer fossil fuels, monitoring our heating and cooling, buying locally, moving toward solar heating and cooling, operating fuel-efficient vehicles, and eating lower on the fuel chain. If we live in the United States, we can begin to live like Europeans, who live comfortably using half the renewable energy sources as North Americans.[55] We can, as Francis did, honor the elements that sustain our lives and prize sustainability over obsolescence. This means loving the nonhuman world with the same care as we have for our children and grandchildren. In fact, as we care for the nonhuman world, we ensure a healthier world for our children. According to his biographers,

When [Francis] washed his hands, he chose a place where water would not be trampled underfoot by his washings. Whenever he had to walk over rocks, he would walk with fear and reverence out of love for him who is called "The Rock." He also told the brother who cut the wood for fire not to cut down the whole tree, but to cut it in such a way that one part remained while the other was cut.... He used to tell the brother who took care of the garden not to cultivate all the ground in the garden for vegetables, but to leave a piece of the ground that would produce wild plants that in their season would produce "Brother Flowers." Moreover, he used to tell the brother gardener that he should make a beautiful flower bed in the same part of the garden, planting and cultivating every variety of fragrant plants and those producing beautiful flowers.[56]

Like Francis, we can put our faith into practice by putting the realm of God, God's *shalom* for all creation, ahead of self-interest, consumption, and competition. We can think and act locally, planting trees and making changes that will last beyond our lifetimes. We can also act and advocate globally for a world in which countries look beyond self-interest and nation-first to embrace the whole earth. Cosmopolitan, earth-affirming spirituality applies to spiritual communities as well as individuals and institutions. Francis challenges our churches to become pioneers in green spirituality, living more simply, reducing the use of fossil fuels in heating and cooling, and supporting environmental initiatives in our communities.

Climate change and the coronavirus pandemic have revealed how intricately we are connected. No nation, congregation, or community can stand alone. We depend on one another for health, happiness, and hope. In the spirit of Francis, we need to initiate a new form of patriotism, which balances love of country with love of the planet and challenges our institutions, private and public, to become the gardeners and healers of the earth and stewards of our children's future.

## FRESH SPIRITUALITY

The quest to refresh creation requires the healing of individuals, institutions, economics, nations, and the planet. In the intricate interdependence of life, we must do multiple things at once, knowing that every action reverberates across the planet, and that earth-affirming people can still hope to be a tipping point from death to life for our planet. For Francis as well as ourselves, the journeys, inner and outer, are simultaneous. In changing ourselves, we take steps to changing the world. We can't wait for others, including politicians and religious leaders, to take the lead.

### Consider the Lilies

Jesus challenged his followers to put God's realm above all else. If we prioritize God's *shalom*, the healing of individuals, nations, and the planet, we will discover that we already have everything we need.

> Look at the birds of the air; they neither sow nor reap nor
> gather into barns, and yet your heavenly Father feeds them.
> Are you not of more value than they? And can any of you
> by worrying add a single hour to your span of life? And
> why do you worry about clothing? Consider the lilies of the
> field, how they grow; they neither toil nor spin, yet I tell
> you, even Solomon in all his glory was not clothed like one
> of these. But if God so clothes the grass of the field, which
> is alive today and tomorrow is thrown into the oven, will he
> not much more clothe you—you of little faith? Therefore
> do not worry, saying, 'What will we eat?' or 'What will we
> drink?' or 'What will we wear?'... But strive first for the
> kingdom of God and his righteousness, and all these things
> will be given to you as well. (Matthew 6:26–31, 33)

In this spiritual examination, consider what role the nonhuman world and God's realm have in your life. Begin your time of spiritual reflection with a time of stillness, asking God for guidance as you look honestly at your values and lifestyle. Then, allow ample time, perhaps over a few days, to consider the following:

• What values determine your day-to-day life, including your
  purchasing and personal attention? Are your daily values and
  economic behaviors congruent with your spiritual beliefs?

- Where do you experience anxiety or stress in your life? Is there any relationship between your daily anxieties and your economic life and time commitments?

- How would your life change if you placed God's realm first? How would this shape your purchases, charitable giving, relationships to family, friends, and strangers? How would it influence your political involvement?

- What one thing can you do, as a first step, to align yourself more fully with God's realm?

- Conclude by giving thanks for the opportunity for self-examination and the ability to change.

*Radical Amazement*

Without wonder at the universe and our planet and its creatures, we can't fully appreciate God's world or express gratitude for God's creative wisdom that brings forth galaxies, planets, people, flora, and fauna.

To inspire amazement, take time each day to read Francis's "Canticle of the Creatures" that introduced this chapter, along with the words of Psalms 148 and 150:6. Place yourself in the universe described by the psalmist and Francis as you experience your day. Pause and notice the world around you—clouds, thunderstorms, morning sun, fireflies and grasshoppers, a running fox and a sleeping dog, the unique faces of the people around you, and the world in all its variety of flora, fauna, winged creatures, and creeping things. Take time to contemplate photos of atoms and cells. Gaze on the photographs from the Webb and Hubble telescopes.

Throughout the day, remind yourself that you are on holy ground. Cultivate reverence of life in your attitudes and actions.

## Simplicity of Spirit

Spiritual simplicity is more important than ever. Francis and Clare sought holy poverty to deepen their relationship with God, align themselves with God's vision for their lives, and experience solidarity with all creation. Holy simplicity reminded them of their dependence on God and interdependence with all creation. We need to embrace these values today. We also need to embrace a fresh simplicity of spirit, reflected in simplicity of life and transformed approaches to economics. We must, as St. Elizabeth Ann Seton asserted, "live simply so others may simply live." More than that, our simplicity of life is essential for planetary survival. We need to declutter our material and spiritual lives, liberating ourselves from consumerism to become God's companions in planetary healing. In this spiritual exercise, take time to consider the following, after a time of prayerful silence and petitionary prayer for God to guide your attitude toward material possessions and consumption.

- How do you evaluate your economic life? Do you have sufficient resources to live comfortably and provide for your own and others' needs and to be generous to causes that are important to you?
- How do you feel about your possessions? Do you feel comfortable with your current level of consumption? Is it appropriate or too much? How does your consumption relate to others' well-being, including the nonhuman world?
- In what ways might you appropriately and safely reduce your consumption of fossil fuels and non-renewable products?
- What changes might you make to live more simply and sustainably?
- Ask for God's guidance in simplifying your life. Ask God to give you wisdom in addressing issues of simplicity with your family and the institutions of which you are a part.

### Fresh Prayer

God of all creation, all creatures great and small,

open my eyes to the wonders of your world and my life.

Help me to pause and notice.

Help me to be aware and amazed,

and share my joy with others.

Help me to live more simply,

to see my consumption in light of the well-being

of others and the planet.

Let me experience the freedom of spiritual and material simplicity

and let me share my wealth to support those in need

and causes that promote justice and planetary healing.

Amen.

CHAPTER EIGHT

# *Creating Peace*

Peace I leave with you; my peace I give to you. I do not give to you as the world gives. Do not let your hearts be troubled, and do not let them be afraid.

—JOHN 14:27

In all his preaching, before he presented the word of God to the assembly, he prayed for peace, saying, "May the Lord give you peace."[57]

—THOMAS OF CELANO

Long before I knew much about Francis of Assisi, I was inspired by the Peace Prayer of St. Francis. My staunchly Protestant mother had a plaque in her bedroom with the words of the prayer accompanied by the painting of a monk. I suspect that my mother, often troubled by anxiety and depression, found great consolation in the prayer she saw as she awakened each morning. Most scholars agree that the prayer that bears the saint's name is actually a twentieth-century expression of his irenic and inclusive spirit:

> Lord, make me an instrument of Your peace;
> Where there is hatred, let me sow love;
> Where there is injury, pardon;
> Where there is doubt, faith;
> Where there is despair, hope;
> Where there is darkness, light;
> And where there is sadness, joy.
> O Divine Master,
> Grant that I may not so much seek
> To be consoled as to console;
> To be understood, as to understand;
> To be loved, as to love;
> For it is in giving that we receive,
> It is in pardoning that we are pardoned,
> And it is in dying that we are born to Eternal Life.
> Amen.

This prayer is dear to my heart. Each morning, as I begin my walk, I repeat the first lines, "Lord, make me an instrument of your peace," along with an affirmation that Francis prescribed for his followers, "This is the day that God has made, let us rejoice and be glad in it." In times of conflict or unease, I recall these words, "Lord, make me an instrument of your peace." I know that I need God's peace, and I cling to Francis's salutation, "May the Lord give you peace," to keep me centered on God despite my own anxieties. I often quietly say these words, "May God give you peace," in times of conflict or when I feel alienated from a companion or someone whom I encounter on social media or cable news. Like Francis and Clare, I recognize that in troubled times, God is my rock and salvation, and that nothing can separate me from the love of God. Peace is not the result of denial or avoidance, nor is it calm amid others' suffering; peace is grounded in the experiences of self-transcendence when we truly believe, as Francis and Clare did, in "God and all things." In that belief, we experience God in our past, present, and future, and in every situation we are inspired to sacrifice self-interest for world loyalty.

Francis and Clare believed that inner and outer peace are connected. A peaceful world is the fruit of individuals committed to peace. When we experience inner peace, we have the courage and trust to embrace holy simplicity and solidarity with others. It brings peace to our families, communities, nation, and planet.

### Peace with the Church

I am sure that Francis knew that his gospel piety would be seen as a threat to the status quo of a wealthy and powerful church. Surely, he was aware of the cardinals and bishops who opposed the formation of his order. Clare may have felt frustrated at the resistance to her request to emphasize poverty in her rule of the

Order of the Poor Ladies. Francis and Clare, nevertheless, persevered. They looked beyond the resistance they faced to see a deeper reality, the ongoing ministry of Christ in the world. They pursued God's call despite the impediments that others placed in their way. Their peace came from self-transcendence.

Today, we have greater access than Francis and Clare to the levers of power within religious and governmental institutions. We are heirs of a democratic spirit that was unheard of in Francis's and Clare's time. When we see an injustice in religious institutions, we believe that we have the duty to respond, whether we are confronting financial misconduct, sexual abuse, white Christian nationalism, or apathy toward issues of justice and environmental care. We must call religious institutions to account when they stray from their ideals and vocations and become instruments of injustice and violence. Francis and Clare remind us, however, that even in the heat of conflict, God is present in the lives of those whose injustices we must challenge. They remind us that the quest for justice heals the souls of oppressor and oppressed alike. We can, in the spirit of Jesus's admonitions:

> Love your enemies and pray for those who persecute you, so that you may be children of your Father in heaven; for he makes his sun rise on the evil and on the good and sends rain on the righteous and on the unrighteous. (Matthew 5:44–45)

Love your enemies, do good to those who hate you, bless those who curse you, pray for those who abuse you. (Luke 6:27–28)

Peacemakers experience God's blessing. They experience the simplicity of heart that reconciles friend and enemy and brings us the peace that passes all understanding.

### Peace with Otherness

Francis's and Clare's world was characterized by violence and division. During the Crusades, Christians and Muslims saw each other as infidels. Sworn enemies, Christians and Muslims believed that killing each other was the guarantee of eternal life. In this time of violence and hatred, Francis crossed boundaries, risking his life and reputation, to engage in spiritual dialogue with Sultan Malik al-Kamil in Damietta, Egypt. Though perceived as "enemies" by their respective religions, Francis and the sultan spoke respectfully to each other as God's beloved children. While the sultan was not persuaded to follow the faith of Jesus, he "was overflowing with admiration and recognized [Francis] as a man unlike any other. He was moved by his words and listened to him very willingly."[58]

Francis went beyond "otherness" in approaching the Muslim political leader. His outreach to Sultan Malik al-Kamil is a model for interfaith relationships in our time, as well as the quest for reconciliation among enemies. Francis spoke and he also listened, suggesting that Christians can learn and grow from relationships with people of other religious traditions. Although our theologies, spiritual practices, and forms of worship differ, we are united as God's beloved children. Francis's vision of a democracy of spirit inspires us to look for truth and beauty everywhere. Wherever truth and healing are found, God is its source, whether in other religious traditions, science laboratories, or critiques from religious "outsiders." Francis's dialogue with the sultan challenges us to welcome the insights and practices of people of other faiths. In a world of division and exclusion, our faith must be cosmopolitan and our actions welcoming and affirming. In relating to people of other faiths, Francis reminds us that we are one in God's Spirit. There is no other.

The ultimate "others" are often the people closest to us. Our life companions, children and grandchildren, siblings, and good friends are reflections of divine creativity, with unique gifts, life histories, traumas and delights, and perspectives and opinions. They are truly our "holy other," in which the meaning of the Southern African term, *ubuntu,* "I am because of you, we are because of each other," is made flesh. More than anyone else, we need God's peace, a sense of self-transcendence, sacrifice, forgiveness, and letting go in relationship to our loved ones. They are often the source of our greatest pain as well as our greatest joy.

When leading his community of friars, Francis was always clear in his expectations and accepted his companions' fallibilities. He related to his companions as individuals who required unique and personal care. No one size fits all in relationships, parenting, marriage, or community life. When Francis saw that his Order of Friars Minor was changing, he resigned his institutional leadership. He remained spiritual leader of the order but recognized that his expectations might be a source of conflict and possibly an impediment to future growth. Francis and Clare never wrote a primer on relationships. Their peace-oriented style of relationship, however, invites us to give others space to grow, withhold unnecessary critique and judgment, recognize our own relational limitations, and always seek the well-being of our "holy others" on their terms, not our own, trusting their lives to God's loving direction.

### Peace with the Planet and Its Creatures

One of the most well-known stories of Francis's life involves his healing relationship with a dangerous wolf who tormented the citizens of the Umbrian village of Gubbio. The townsfolk of Gubbio had been terrorized by a vicious predator for many years, to the point that they were afraid to go out into the countryside without weaponry. They sent out hunting parties without success and the wolf continued to terrorize the village, frightening children and attacking sheep. The lover of creation, human and nonhuman, Francis sought a resolution to this deadly conflict. To the villagers' horror, Francis sought out the wolf. When the wolf saw Francis, the vicious creature charged at him but stopped in his tracks when Francis made the sign of the cross and then admonished the wolf for his violent behavior. To the amazement of onlookers, the unarmed friar challenged the wolf to claim the path of peace, demanding that it refrain from attacking the townspeople and their domestic animals. Deep down, the wolf realized that he had a higher destiny than killing and terrorizing. When Francis returned to the village, he gave the wary villagers a similar command: to welcome the wolf and ensure that he was fed and cared for. The once-vicious wolf and the once-frightened villagers experienced a conversion of heart, recognizing their common identity as God's creatures and learning to live in peace.

Peace eludes the majority of humankind. We are alienated from nature and from one another. The planet is in jeopardy because human beings, viewing themselves as outsiders unrelated to the rest of creation, see the nonhuman world as a resource for profit-making. We have gained the world, but we are in danger of losing not only our souls but also the lives of future generations. Every morning's news testifies to our alienation from one another. Nations threaten war, racism puts national unity at risk, and incivility marks our daily social media activity and political action. We need peace, the peace that comes from within and calms and reconciles a troubled and divided planet.

Francis counseled his followers to have this affirmation on their lips in every encounter: "May the peace of the Lord be with you." In his world of conflict, violence, and social and economic division, the pilgrimage to peace was undertaken one step and one word at a time. Francis realized that peace emerges when we overcome the fears that separate us. Living simply, with nothing to protect, we discover our deeper connection with our human and nonhuman kin. We are not other; we are kinfolk. A Central American mother fleeing to the United States with her children in search of safety cares for her children with the same passion as a mother taking her children to school in my Washington, DC, suburb. Soldiers on the battlefield simply want to get home safe and sound to their families and ensure their nation's survival. Right whale pups and kittens rejoice in waking up to a new day and so do my grandchildren.

For every peacemaker, there is a deeper unity, beneath our diversity and conflict. God moves through all of our lives, and if we listen, we will hear the heartbeat of God's love in every creature—friend and foe, human and nonhuman. Although we may choose solitude, there is no aloneness. Although we have differing gifts, there is a more primordial unity that binds us. Although our aspirations may at times appear to be at cross-purposes, deep down we are connected, inspired by the hope of love, happiness, and a better life for our families.

Francis did not describe the steps to peace and reconciliation. He simply lived peacefully, letting peace guide his words and actions. He left the details of peacemaking among families, communities, religious and ethnic groups, species, and nations to us, believing that when peace is our goal, we will find our way one step and encounter at a time. We will trust that God's peace is always ours and that we have nothing to fear when we choose to say, "The peace of the Lord be with you."

### Peace with Aging, Diminishment, and Death

At a recent Bible study, I asked members of my class, all of whom were over sixty, the pointed question, "When you read about the death of a celebrity or politician, do you ever think 'how many years do I have to go to reach that age'?" All of my Zoom study group members raised their hands. The baby boomers and the remaining members of the greatest generation have come to realize that they are mortal. Death is the one thing we can't fix. The mortality rate will remain 100 percent regardless of our technology, good fortune, or healthy habits. This reality was graphic during the first year of the COVID-19 pandemic, when many members of the Medicare generation assessed their risk factors and worried that one cough or unwashed hand might spiral into a ventilator and a memorial service. Moreover, as we age, we worry about dementia, Alzheimer's disease, physical incapacity, and the loneliness that follows the death of our loved ones.

Francis and Clare lived in a time in which death could not be denied. Life expectancy hovered between thirty and forty years of age. The Crusades, like all wars, carried off young adults, touching directly or indirectly almost every family in Italy. Francis and Clare both suffered from chronic ailments that daily reminded them of the fragility of life. Francis's first awakening to God's call in his life came during a time of convalescence as he began to question his aspirations to be a knight and discovered a path to a realm whose Sovereign had the keys to true happiness and everlasting life.

In his final years, Francis experienced intimacy with Jesus when God granted him the gift of the stigmata, the wounds of the crucified Christ. The stigmata opened Francis further to God's care for the world, revealed in Jesus's suffering love. In experiencing Jesus's pain, Francis sanctified his own pain and diminishment. He realized that nothing could separate him from the suffering and joyful love of God. Even in physical pain, he could reach out to others in compassion and share his final gifts of wisdom and love. Perhaps he realized that fresh spirituality, the faith that is ever new and ever beginning again, is a constant process of letting go and dying and rising with Christ.

Francis's experience of the stigmata was the prelude to his final earthly adventure. As his life force waned, he asked his physician how much time he had left. When the physician revealed that death was imminent, Francis lifted his hands to the heavens and cried out, "Welcome, Sister Death!"

Francis died with words of praise on his lips, knowing that whether he lived or died, he was surrounded by the One whose center is everywhere and whose circumference is nowhere. As Francis breathed his last, a flock of larks alighted on the monastery roof and begin chanting hymns of praise, joining their grief with gratitude for God's presence in Francis's life. With the apostle Paul, Francis and his creaturely companions proclaimed, "Where, O death, is your victory? Where, O death, is your sting?" (1 Corinthians 15:55). Francis had made peace with death, knowing that Sister Death is the doorway to life everlasting.

Clare felt that same confidence in God's everlasting love. Her commitment to simplicity was a preparation for death and eternal life, not a flight from the alone to the Alone, or a denial of embodiment, but an opening to eternity. Clare counseled, "Place your mind in the mirror of eternity! Place your soul in the brilliance of glory."[59] Moreover, "if you suffer with Him, you shall reign with Him, [if you] weep [with Him], you will rejoice with Him, [if you] die [with Him] on the cross of tribulation, you shall possess heavenly mansions in the splendor of the saints."[60]

Clare affirmed, "O Blessed Poverty, who bestows eternal riches on those who love and embrace her."[61]

Francis and Clare inspire us to live each day knowing that "this is the day that God has made." Each day is unique and unrepeatable. Each day is the meeting place of life and death, and time and eternity. Seize the day! Put first things first. Moving forward means letting go of the limitations of the past and welcoming the fresh possibilities of this present moment and new beginnings of the future. Don't lose an opportunity to awaken to God's vision for your life and share your love to others. In holy simplicity, we die to the finite, defended self, and join with the Self of the universe. Then we can joyfully proclaim, "May the peace of God be with you, for it is in dying that we are born to eternal life."

## FRESH SPIRITUALITY

Francis's greeting "May the Lord give you peace" is more than a slogan. It is a way of life, grounded in the affirmation "God and all things." God's universal care inspires us to self-transcendence, to simplify our lives for the greater good and planetary survival, and to go from self-interest to world loyalty. We jettison the small, defensive self to embrace the unity of ourselves with God's Self. We experience the peace of Christ which enables us to face conflict, threat, and death, knowing that our lives and all creation are in God's care.

*Let Peace Begin with Me*

I grew up singing, "Let there be peace on earth and let it begin with me." Liberation theologians remind us that the personal is political and the political is personal. Francis and Clare would say that the journey inward and outward are connected. Inner peace leads to peaceful behaviors, whether we are parents, citizens, or presidents. As I wrote this chapter, I used "Let There Be Peace on Earth" as a writing prompt, listening to versions as varied as Vince Gill, a children's choir serenading Pope Francis, and Sweet Honey in the Rock. I invite you to do the same. Let the various versions soak in, shaping your daily experience. Take time throughout the day to affirm one of the following statements, "Let peace on earth begin with me" or "God, make me an instrument of your peace." Let this affirmation be a talisman, bringing you back to your spiritual center whenever you are tempted to lash out in anger or disparage another person. Make a commitment to be a peacemaker wherever you find yourself.

*Peace Walking*

When I was growing up in the Salinas Valley in California, visitors often appeared at our parsonage, looking for places to stay or handouts. My generous pastor-father let migrant workers sleep in our garage and my mom always put together a plate of sandwiches for people in need. One summer, a young man named Wes came by the church seeking shelter for the night. He was walking from Los Angeles to San Francisco for world peace and nuclear disarmament. My father gave him a place at the church to sleep, and that night after dinner, he played folk songs on his guitar by the Kingston Trio, Pete Seeger, and Peter, Paul, and Mary.

Years later, in college, I met a woman known as Peace Pilgrim. In the 1940s, a successful businesswoman named Mildred Lisette Norman (1908–1981) felt a yearning for something more. In the early 1950s, she took a sabbatical to walk the Appalachian Trail. In course of that walking, she had a mystical experience that changed the course of her life. She legally changed her name to Peace Pilgrim, sold her possessions, and acquired a simple tunic that read "Peace Pilgrim." She began her pilgrimage for peace on January 1, 1953, and walked every day for the next twenty-eight years. Like Francis of Assisi, she carried no money, refused contributions, often slept outdoors, and depended on the grace of strangers for meals and lodging.[62]

In this spiritual practice, commit yourself to walking each day for peace. Begin your walk with an affirmation, such as "Let there be peace on earth" or "God, make me an instrument of peace." Gently repeat the words "peace, peace, peace," to center your spirit and add to the peace of the planet. When you encounter someone, consider saying silently or aloud, "God give you peace." I believe that our invocation of these words and a conscious commitment to being peacemakers creates a spiritual force field around us that not only protects our spirits but also brings peace and healing to our relationships and environment.

*Beyond Hiroshima*

Every August, I read John Hersey's *Hiroshima* to remind me of the continuing threat of nuclear war. Sometimes a typographical error reveals a deep truth. In writing a piece on Hiroshima Day, I had intended to write "mutually assured destruction" to describe the current policy of deterrence practiced by the atomic superpowers. Instead, I typed "mutually assumed destruction." Perhaps, unconsciously, I was rattled by threats by the leaders of two atomic powers that they might, if pushed to it, use atomic weapons to protect their nations and destroy any neighboring country.

Although Francis and Clare couldn't imagine nuclear armaments, they knew the cost of national and regional violence. They sought an alternative through the pathway of peace, which led Francis to reach out to Sultan Malik al-Kamil. Francis and Clare would have recognized even in the time of the Crusades that there is no such thing as foreign policy in isolation from the rest of our lives. What happens beyond our borders shapes our own community's experience. Initially, Francis's military experience predisposed him to war as a solution to political conflicts.

After his encounters with Jesus, Francis realized that the only way to peace is to be peaceful and to seek peace. Franciscan spirituality does not provide clear answers or strategies in the quest for peace. It would, however, challenge the leaders of world to put as much effort into peacemaking as warmongering.

"Blessed are the peacemakers," proclaim followers of Jesus, Francis, and Clare. The quest for peace in international politics can involve activities as varied as encouraging political leaders and representatives to make peacemaking a priority; divesting from war-related investments; supporting veterans dealing with emotional, physical, and moral trauma or injury, and the simple act of daily praying for peace among the nations, especially those nations that are perceived as our country's enemies.

*Peace with Diminishment and Death*

No one can escape aging and death. Even Francis and Clare spiritually and emotionally struggled with their chronic illnesses and dying processes. In this spiritual practice, I invite you to prayerfully recite the following spiritual affirmations as reminders that we are always in God's hands. You may choose to reflect on these passages in the spirit of *lectio divina*, or holy reading, opening to the word or phrase that inspires you, repeating it and asking God's guidance to embody your insights as you face diminishment and death.

For we do not live to ourselves, and we do not die to ourselves. If we live, we live to the Lord, and if we die, we die to the Lord; so then, whether we live or whether we die, we are the Lord's. For to this end Christ died and lived again, so that he might be Lord of both the dead and the living. (Romans 14:7–9)

For I am convinced that neither death, nor life, nor angels, nor rulers, nor things present, nor things to come, nor powers, nor height, nor depth, nor anything else in all creation will be able to separate us from the love of God in Christ Jesus our Lord. (Romans 8:38–39)

Where can I go from your spirit?
Or where can I flee from your presence?
If I ascend to heaven, you are there;
if I make my bed in Sheol, you are there.
If I take the wings of the morning
and settle at the farthest limits of the sea,
even there your hand shall lead me,
and your right hand shall hold me fast.
If I say, "Surely the darkness shall cover me,
and the light around me become night,"
even the darkness is not dark to you;
the night is as bright as the day,
for darkness is as light to you. (Psalm 139:7–12)

Give thanks each day for the gift of life and the opportunities each day brings. Live each day with a spirit of novelty, freshness, and new beginnings, for "this is the day that God has made."

## FRESH PRAYER

God, make me an instrument of peace.

Let my thoughts, words, and actions

bring peace to the world.

Let me speak peacefully to my significant others

and all I encounter.

Let me be an instrument of peace in my citizenship,

praying for our nation's leaders as well as our nation's enemies.

Let peace be every step.

Amen.

CHAPTER NINE

# *Always New, Always Fresh, Always Beginning Again*

So if anyone is in Christ, there is a new creation: everything old has passed away; see, everything has become new!

—2 CORINTHIANS 5:17

Francis was always new, always fresh, always beginning again.

—THOMAS OF CELANO

Although Clare counseled her companions to gaze, consider, contemplate, and imitate Christ, she knew that God invited her to embody a unique form of discipleship as a woman in the thirteenth century. Described as the "perfect Christian," Francis recognized that his imitation of Jesus, his quest to have the mind of Christ, was unique to his time of Crusades, church wealth and power, and feudalism, and he could not replicate a life in

Roman-occupied first-century Judea. Francis and Clare gave up power and privilege. Most of the early followers of Jesus had no power or property. Accordingly, Francis and Clare would forgo privileges unavailable to the least of these.

Spirituality is always concrete. Our embrace of Francis's and Clare's vision, and our commitment to holy poverty, takes place in the twenty-first century, a world vastly different than that of the Franciscan founders. We read books, spend hours on the internet, communicate on social media, travel the globe, and have investments, retirement accounts, and health care plans. We encounter religious and cultural pluralism on a daily basis. We study Francis and Lao Tzu, the Dalai Lama, and Gautama Buddha. We find peace of mind through meditation and medication. Yet, like Francis and Clare, we realize that our world is in upheaval. We can't count on the survival of the old order and wonder what the new order will be. The keys of life and death are in our hands. Simplicity of life is a matter of ecological survival and care for future generations as well as a path to experience God more fully. The twelfth- and thirteenth-century carnage of the Crusades and inter-city wars has given way to the potentially unlimited destruction of twenty-first-century nuclear war. Our encounters with Francis, Clare, and Franciscan spirituality must integrate ancient and present wisdom and practice. Yesterday's spirituality was not sufficient for the early Franciscans, nor is it sufficient for us. Francis was always new, always fresh, always beginning again. We must embrace the same creative transformation of past spirituality in light of the demands and possibilities of our time. We must embody a new kind of countercultural foolishness for the twenty-first century.

There is no clear road map ahead for us as we forge new paths. Clare's quest to write the rule of her order was not approved until she was facing her own death. Francis didn't know what would happen, and he was prepared for martyrdom, when he crossed into enemy territory to share Christ with an Egyptian sultan. We must march forward, guided by the light of God, the crucified Christ, and our "good ancestors," among them Clare, Francis, and Bonaventure.

Whether living in a monastery like Clare or on the road like Francis, we must seek to be Christ's pilgrims in our time, living out the message of peace, simplicity, solidarity, inclusiveness, creativity, and healing of our church and our world. Francis and Clare, following the guideposts of Jesus, point the way toward a radiant spiritual future, embracing people and planet. We are not alone. God is with us. Jesus charts the way. The spirit of Francis, Clare, and Bonaventure faithfully guides us in all times and places, even beyond Christianity, providing guidance to seekers everywhere. We embrace one another in the graceful interdependence of life.

The path of simplicity and solidarity is part of a greater path, the holy adventure of God, beckoning us to journey forward to God's *shalom.* May the peace of God, Christ, Spirit, and Love be with you!

1. Thomas of Celano, "First Life of St. Francis," in Marion Habig, *St. Francis of Assisi: Omnibus of Sources* (Cincinnati: Franciscan Media, 2009), 118.

2. Thomas of Celano, "First Life of St. Francis," 118.

3. For more on the spiritual journeys of Clare and Bonaventure, see Ilia Delio, *Clare of Assisi: A Heart Full of Love* (Cincinnati: Franciscan Media, 2007); *Simply Bonaventure: An Introduction to His Life, Thought, and Writings* (Hyde Park, NY: New City Press, 2001); *The Humility of God: A Franciscan Perspective* (Cincinnati: St. Anthony Messenger Press, 2005); and *Crucified Love: Bonaventure's Mysticism of the Crucified Christ* (Cincinnati: Franciscan Media, 1998).

4. Bonaventure, *Bonaventure: The Soul's Journey to God*, translated by Ewart Cousins (Mahwah, NJ: Paulist Press, 1968), 5, 8, 100.

5. *Bonaventure: The Soul's Journey to God*, 5, 8, 100.

6. *Bonaventure: The Soul's Journey to God*, 107.

7. Quoted in Ilia Delio, *The Humility of God: A Franciscan Perspective* (Cincinnati: St. Anthony Messenger Press, 2005), 43.

8. *Bonaventure: The Soul's Journey to God*, 148-149. (Inclusive language in the spirit of Francis and Clare.)

9. Regis J. Armstrong and Ignatius C. Brady, *Francis and Clare: The Complete Works* (Mahwah, NJ: Paulist Press, 1982), 200.

10. Albert Schweitzer, *Albert Schweitzer: The Essential Writings* (Maryknoll, NY: Orbis Books, 2005), 73.

11. Schweitzer, 19.

12. Schweitzer, 41.

13. *Francis of Assisi, Early Documents: The Saint*, Volume 1, edited by Regis J. Armstrong, Wayne Hellman, and William Short (Hyde Park: New City Press, 1999), 185.

14. Bonaventure, *Major Life of St. Francis*, in Marion Habig, *St. Francis of Assisi: Omnibus of Sources*, I:3 .

15. *Francis of Assisi, Early Documents: The Saint*, 201-202.

16. Bonaventure, *Major Life of St. Francis*, XI:1

17. Brother Ugolino, *The Little Flowers of St. Francis*, in Marion Habig, *St.*

*Francis of Assisi: Omnibus of Sources*, 7-8.

18. These designations are identified by theologian and New Testament scholar Marcus Borg. See Marcus Borg and N. T. Wright, *The Meaning of Jesus: Two Visions* (San Francisco: HarperOne, 2007).

19. *Francis and Clare: The Complete Works*, 197.

20. For a reflection on Benedictine spirituality, see Norvene Vest, *Preferring Christ: A Devotional Commentary on the Rule of St. Benedict* (Harrisburg, PA: Morehouse Press, 2004).

21. *Francis of Assisi, Early Documents: The Saint*, 229.

22. Harry James Cargas and Bernard Lee, *Religious Experience and Process Theology* (Mahwah, NJ: Paulist Press. 1976), 70.

23. Delio, *Clare of Assisi: A Heart Full of Love*, 71.

24. Delio, *Clare of Assisi: A Heart Full of Love*, 71.

25. *Francis and Clare: The Complete Works*, 192.

26. See Ilia Delio, Keith Douglass Warner, and Pamela Wood, *Care for Creation: A Franciscan Spirituality of the Earth* (Cincinnati: Franciscan Media, 2007).

27. Omer Englebert, *Francis of Assisi: A Biography* (Cincinnati: Franciscan Media, 2013), 32-33.

28. Englebert, *Francis of Assisi*, 32-33.

29. Bonaventure, *Major Life of St. Francis, III:2.*

30. Bonaventure, *Major Life of St. Francis, XIII:2.*

31. *Francis of Assisi: The Saint*, 283.

32. *Francis and Clare: The Complete Works*, 197.

33. *Francis and Clare: The Complete Works*, 200.

34. Bonaventure, *Major Life of St. Francis, II:1.*

35. Bonaventure, *Major Life of St. Francis, X:7.*

36. Omer Englebert, *St, Francis of Assisi: A Biography,* 61-71.

37. Leonardo Boff, *Francis of Assisi* (Maryknoll, NY: Orbis, 1982), 43-44.

38. Boff, *Francis of Assisi ,* 55.

39. Dorothy Day, *The Long Loneliness,* (New York: HarperOne, 2009), 78.

40. Dorothy Day, *On Pilgrimage* (Grand Rapids: Wm. B. Eerdmans, 1999), 5.

41. Dorothy Day, *On Pilgrimage*, 33.

42. Dorothy Day, *On Pilgrimage*, 86.

43. Murray Bodo, *Francis: The Journey and the Dream* (Cincinnati, OH: Franciscan Media, 2011), 169-170.

44. Greta Thunberg, *This I Believe: On Truth, Courage, and Saving Our Planet* (San Francisco: Blackwell and Ruth, 2020), 20.

45. Thunberg, 27.

46. Cindy Wooden, "Pope Francis Explains Why He Chose Francis of Assisi's Name," *Catholic News Service,* 17 March 2013. Quoted in David Ray Griffin, *Protecting Our Common Home: Pope Francis and Process Thought* (Anoka, MN: Process Century Press, 2016), 9.

47. Jack Wintz, OFM , "St Francis of Assisi: Why He's the Patron Saint of Ecology," *St. Anthony Messenger,* October 2007. Quoted in Griffin, *Protecting Our Common Home,* 9.

48. Wintz, 9-10.

49. *Francis of Assisi: Early Documents: The Saint,* 234-236, 250-251.

50. *Francis of Assisi: Early Documents: The Saint,* 251.

51. *Encyclical Letter of the Holy Father Francis, Laudato Si' On Care for Our Common Home* 3.

52. *Laudato Si',* 56, 61.

53. *Francis and Clare: The Complete Works,* 192.

54. *Francis and Clare: The Complete Works,* 193.

55. Ilia Delio, Keith Douglas Warner, Pamela Wood, *Care for Creation: A Franciscan Spirituality of the Earth* (Cincinnati: Franciscan Media, 2018), 186-188.

56. *Francis of Assisi, Early Documents: The Saint,* Volume 2, edited by Regis J. Armstrong, Wayne Hellman, and William Short (Hyde Park: New City Press, 1999), 192.

57. *Francis of Assisi: The Saint,* 200.

58. *Francis of Assisi: The Saint,* 231.

59. *Francis and Clare: The Complete Works,* 200.

60. *Francis and Clare: The Complete Works,* 197.

61. *Francis and Clare: The Complete Works,* 192.

62. For more about Peace Pilgrim, see Bruce Epperly, *Mystics in Action: Twelve Saints for Today* (Maryknoll, NY: Orbis Books, 2020), 90-99.

ABOUT THE AUTHOR

Rev. Dr. Bruce G. Epperly served as a congregational pastor, university chaplain, professor, and seminary administrator for over forty years. He is the author of more than seventy books on practical theology, ministry, and spirituality, healing and wholeness, and process theology, including *Walking with Francis of Assisi: From Privilege to Activism, The Elephant is Running: Process and Open and Relational Theology and Religious Pluralism, The Mystic in You: Discovering a God-filled World,* the award-winning *Tending to the Holy: The Practice of the Presence of God in Ministry,* and *Mystics in Action: Twelve Saints for Today.* He lives in Potomac, Maryland, with his wife Rev. Dr. Katherine Gould Epperly, where he continues to teach, write, and pastor in his retirement, and daily cares for his grandchildren.